South Africa and United Nations Peacekeeping Offensive Operations:

Conceptual Models

Antonio Garcia

Mwanaka Media and Publishing Pvt Ltd,
Chitungwiza Zimbabwe
*
Creativity, Wisdom and Beauty

Publisher:

Mmap

Mwanaka Media and Publishing Pvt Ltd

24 Svosve Road, Zengeza 1

Chitungwiza Zimbabwe

mwanaka@yahoo.com

https//mwanakamediaandpublishing.weebly.com

Distributed in and outside N. America by African Books Collective

orders@africanbookscollective.com

www.africanbookscollective.com

ISBN: 978-0-7974-9441-1

EAN: 9780797494411

DISCLAIMER

All views expressed in this publication are those of the author and do not necessarily reflect the views of *Mmap*

Dedication

I dedicate this book to my wife and partner, Tara Lyle, who loves and supports me in all things.

Acknowledgments

I would like to thank Colonel Andrew Dinwoodie, Lieutenant Colonel Barnard and Professor/Lieutenant Colonel Abel Esterhuyse for their guidance. Much of this work has been the result of my research as a visiting scholar at *New York University (NYU), Center on International Cooperation (CIC)*. Thank you to Sarah Cliff, Jim Della-Giocoma and Paige Arthur for the opportunity to be a part of CIC. I am also grateful to the senior fellows, visiting professors and my fellow visiting scholars at the CIC. Hanny Megally, Kiwako Tanaka, Said Sabir Ibrahimi, Alexis Guidotti, Jacob Udo-Udo Jacob, Michael Harsch, and Jason Stearns– thank you for all your support.

I would like to extend my sincere gratitude to the *Small Wars Journal* for providing an initial platform for me to publish and test my thoughts and ideas on UN offensive peacekeeping. Thank you to the South African Army and the Engineer Corps, UN Mine Action Service, UN Office of Military Affairs, military practitioners and theorists who commented on, supported and or challenged my approach. My gratitude to the South African Army Vision Team and in particular Colonel Laetitia Olivier and Captain Marius Whittle for helping and guiding my thoughts and research.

It was a pleasure to be able to work in MONUSCO with the North Kivu Brigade as well as the Force Intervention Brigade 2014-2015. A special thanks to Colonel Neeraj Pandey. A word of thanks to Professor Ian Van Der Waag, David Katz and Evert Kleynhans. Thank you to Ruth Woudstra for your editorial assistance.

As this is a work of military theory I would like to declare that I understand that the United Nations and many other international organisations abide by the mantra of protection under the leadership of the Secretary General. Where I do believe in its importance, the military must always prepare for war and operations other than war, in whichever way its new character may take shape.

Table of Contents

Acronyms

ASF: Africa Standby Force
ACIRC: African Capacity for Immediate Response to Crises
AU: African Union
ADF: Allied Democratic Forces
FARDC: Armed Forces of the Democratic Republic of the Congo
APLA: Azanian People's Liberation Army
CAR: Central African Republic
CONOPS: Concept of Operations
COE: Contingent Owned Equipment
CCW: Convention on Certain Conventional Weapons
COE: Contingent Owned Equipment
DDR: Demobilisation Disarmament and Reintegration
DFS: Department of Field Support
DIRCO: Department of International Relations and Cooperation
DPKO: Department of Peacekeeping Operations
FDLR: Democratic Forces for the Liberation of Rwanda
DRC: Democratic Republic of the Congo
EOD: Explosive Ordinance Disposal
ERW: Explosive Remnants of War
FIB: Force Intervention Brigade
GDP: Gross Domestic Product
HIPPO: High-Level Independent Panel on UN Peace Operations
IEDs: Improvised Explosive Devices
IHL: International Humanitarian Law
LRA: Lord's Resistance Army
LoC: Lines of Communications
OOW: Operations Other than War

OAU:Organisation of African Unity
POC:Protection of Civilians
MoU: Memorandum of Understanding
MEC: Military Engineer Company
NEPAD: New Partnership for African Development
NGO: Non-Governmental Organisations
PAC: Pan Africanist Congress
SA: South Africa
SAACC: SA Army Capstone Concept
SAAFDSCS: SA Army Future Deployment Strategy Concept System
SAAFOC: SA Army Future Operating Concept
SAASP: The SA Army Strategic Profile
SAAF: South African Air Force
SADF: South African Defence Force
SADC: South African Development Community
SANDF: South African National Defence Force
SRSG: Special Representatives of the Secretary General
TTPs: Tactics, Techniques and Procedures
TCCs: Troop Contributing Countries
MK: uMkhonto we Sizwe
USG: Under Secretary-General
UN: United Nations
UNAMID: United Nations African Union Hybrid Mission in Darfur
UNHQ: United Nations Headquarters
ONUB: United Nations Operation in Burundi
UNMAS: United Nations Mine Action Service
UNSC: United Nations Security Council
MONUC: UN Organisation Mission in the DRC
MINUSCA: UN Multidimensional Integrated Stabilisation Mission in CAR

MINUSMA: UN Multidimensional Integrated Stabilisation Mission in Mali
MONUSCO: UN Stabilisation Mission in the Democratic Republic of the Congo
SDG: UN Sustainable Development Goals
UXO: Unexploded Ordinance

Introduction

This book is a work of military theory. It aims to address current and future conceptual questions about conflict and force employment for the South African (SA) military and the United Nations Department of Peacekeeping Operations (DPKO) in those instances where it takes an offensive role. The United Nations has for the first time mandated offensive peacekeeping operations. This comes at a time when Troop Contributing Countries (TCCs) are increasingly exposed to complex and challenging security contexts.

This work provides an analysis of South Africa's approach to missions and the United Nations Stabilisation Mission in the Democratic Republic of the Congo (MONUSCO). It proposes a conceptual model for force generation and force employment. MONUSCO is currently the only UN offensively mandated peacekeeping operation. The Force Intervention Brigade (FIB) is the sharp tactical component of MONUSCO tasked with the neutralising of armed groups. South Africa is a TCC, and thus holds a key strategic role in achieving the mission's objectives.

The FIB came about as a regional response from sub-Saharan African powers opposing the Rwanda backed M23 rebel military group. South Africa, Tanzania and Malawi were the TCCs which dedicated their fighting forces to neutralise the M23. The 2013 operations against the M23 were a success, and added weight to the political decision to intervene in the Eastern Democratic Republic of the Congo (DRC). The African Union (AU) did not have the financial or logistical resources to deploy forces by itself. As a result, the FIB was placed within MONUSCO.

The FIB responded well in defeating the M23. However, there has been a considerable amount of critique about its less successful military actions against the Democratic Forces for the Liberation of Rwanda (FDLR), the Allied Democratic Forces (ADF), and the Lord's Resistance Army (LRA). The neutralising of M23 was for the most part regarded as a political objective for regional African powers. The subsequent United Nations Security Council (UNSC) mandated objectives were to defeat the ADF, FDLR and LRA. These objectives were perhaps not regarded with equal importance by the African states, who had an initial interest in preventing the M23 from gaining a foothold in the Eastern DRC. A strategic disconnect therefore exists between the political will of the nation states that have been deployed, and the mandate of the UNSC.

The aim of this work is to provide a conceptual model for South African military future operations and force generation and force application in UN offensive peacekeeping operations. The main role of the South African National Defence Force (SANDF) is conventional operations and territorial protection. Its secondary purpose is the provision of forces for deployment in peacekeeping and Operations Other than War (OOW) within sub-Saharan Africa. The central premise of this work finds its existence at the nexus of the SANDF and UN military conceptual models for operational application. It is thus integral to planning for future operations.

In this undertaking, a layer of military and Clausewitzian theory is added to offensive peacekeeping operations. This model involves the primacy of politics but requires an in-depth understanding of the military aspect which is essential in achieving strategic objectives. Peacekeeping missions are often characterised by a disconnect between the politico-strategic and field level.

The cultural complexity between certain nation states and organisations has led to inertia in the conduct of operations. These organisations include but are not limited to the UN, the AU and the militaries of the various TCCs. This point is very technical, and is thus often a theme which is not discussed for preference of a macro-approach. This outlook may focus the higher order aspects of international relations such as political interest and caveats, the pillars of peace building, prevention and sustainable development, and regional cooperation among others. Where it is important to focus on macro-themes. Yet they have the tendency to leave an operational gap for practitioners at the tactical level. The task of strategic guidance thus falls to political, military and strategic theorists who must understand the macro politico-strategic dimension as well as the tactical sphere regarding the very practical matters of boots on the ground.

The macro and micro level aspects of peacekeeping should of course not be mutually exclusive, but part of a comprehensive whole. This work thus aims to introduce a conceptual model for planning future peacekeeping missions in Africa through the lens of the SANDF. Furthermore, the book offers a model for UN offensive peacekeeping operations. A central idea in this work is that there should be continuity between the UN's peacekeeping conceptual models for operational application, force generation and employment, and that of the respective TCCs.

Peacekeeping is in many ways the art of the dialectic. There exists, however, a divide between the civilian and military spheres in operations and at the Headquarters of the United Nations (UNHQ – from here onwards referred to as 'HQ'). There is a further division between the HQ and field operations. It stands to reason that if there is a rupture between field and HQ civilian staff, an even greater gap would exist between civilian staff at HQ and military staff in the field. Moreover, there are fissures in the field between military personnel and civilians.

In general, we fear what we do not know and there are many unknowns between military and civilian staff as well as grey areas and blind spots between HQ and field staff. Within the complexities of peacekeeping missions, the disparity between uniformed and non-uniformed personnel remains a matter of concern. Divergent views are often held by the various groupings, and stereotyping tends to occur. Military personnel involved in peacekeeping are often regarded as lazy and unresponsive, with a laisser-faire attitude. They may also be seen as having a disregard for and lack of knowledge of their particular context. On the other hand, UN civilian staff are frequently viewed by militaries as amateurish and lacking a sense of leadership, decision making abilities and management skills. The perceptions are largely based on inadequate knowledge and appreciation of the other's role and function within the mission. Both parties play an integral role in peacekeeping missions. The mission could therefore perform more efficiently by promoting a greater understanding of the other's purpose.

Another discrepancy that exists is the use of force in missions, which contrasts in many ways with the general mantra of prevention, which has pervaded the UN and the international research industry which surrounds the Secretariat. The concept of preventing future conflict is in no way a new one. It goes without saying that the establishment of the UN and its predecessor – the League of Nations – were found on this very concept. The critical difference is that the international security context has changed considerably.

In comparison the early 20th century, small wars are currently more prevalent. There is an increased potential for many failed states to harbour terrorists and become hubs for foreign extremist ideologies. Economic exploitation by multinational and criminal elements has also become a significant factor. It is often in complex security environments, where UN peacekeeping missions are mandated to carry out operations that peace treaties, agreements of power sharing, elections, corruption and ongoing conflict occur at once.

Ongoing low level conflict is the cause and effect of continued instability in many regions in Africa. Where there is insufficient economic means and political representation of the people – as well as relative deprivation and generational cycles of violence – there are often flare ups of brutal conflict. This reaction is a common occurrence in human history. Prevention is a noble and very important vision for the UN. But there are also dedicated peacekeepers on the ground who deal with a very different reality on a day to day basis. This work in no way aims to diminish the importance of prevention and the UN Sustainable Development Goals (SDG). Rather, it aims to incorporate the practicalities of war, conflict and violence in the broader discussion of peace and security. Our understanding of the contemporary security moment tends to be largely based on our knowledge of conflict during the 20th century and the general western academic and social disdain for the military following the World Wars.

Georges Clemenceau, Prime Minister of France during the First World War, was quoted as saying, "War is too important to be left to the generals." These words were spoken at a time when there were very real fears for personal and national security. These were very likely the thoughts of a leader who had ideas about how to advise on the fight, with the hopes of achieving a better end.

The First World War was an example of the escalation of hostilities which combined the arms race with technological development and antiquated political systems. These pitched Empire and nation state against each other for the sake of imperial objectives. The systems of treaties locked various empires and states into war. Following the First World War, the objective of the League of Nations was to prevent further major conflict. During the Second World War, however, for the majority of belligerents there was an overwhelming public support for the War. The Second World War, being a true industrial and total war, had a cataclysmic effect on the modern world. It consequently also led to a widespread repulsion of War and conflict in its aftermath.

The objectives of the League of Nations were similar to those of its successor, the UN. Both have aimed to keep the world at peace. The League of Nations spoke about disarmament (the modern form being Demobilisation Disarmament and Reintegration (DDR) and solving conflict through negotiation. The current permanent membership of the Security Council (SC) is based on the original version of the League. This group of nations were the victors of the First World War and the Second World War. In modern times, the SC is forced to negotiate a complex and constantly changing security context in war torn states with limited international interest and support.

Public support from respective nation states in deploying their soldiers to peacekeeping operations as blue helmets is normally low. These missions frequently take place in challenging contexts, often in failed or failing states with some amount of violent conflict. As a result, many first world countries refrain from deploying their forces as blue helmets. This marks a stark contrast to many Western countries being TCCs 25 years ago. Various difficult and challenging missions and failures, such as those in Rwanda and Srebrenica, have resulted in many First World countries no longer wishing to contribute blue helmets to complex and dangerous peacekeeping missions. As a lesser option, many Western countries opt for triangular training, and resource and financial support to missions and the DPKO. Public opinion in the various nation states that deploy peacekeepers is often neutral. This impartiality is frequently based on the condition that there are limited casualties. In South Africa, a similar approach exists. The majority of the population is neutral on the topic of peacekeeping and military application on the African continent.

It was Thabo Mbeki, the second democratically elected president of South Africa, who pushed forward the vision and agenda of the African renaissance. This concept was first captured in writing by the Senegalese historian and anthropologist Cheikh Anta Diop in a collection of essays and works on the politics and history of Africa, "Towards the African Renaissance: Essays in African Culture and Development, 1946-1960". In the late 1990s, Mbeki took this concept and launched it on the international stage through a number of speeches. He then led the reorganisation of the Organisation of African Unity (OAU) and converted it into the AU. The South African military was tasked with a new mission in the training, preparation and projection of forces in sub-Saharan Africa. Its objective was to promote peace and stability. In addition to its territorial defence and sovereignty, and deployment in AU and UN peace missions, the newly formed South African military had found a new purpose.

The South African political vision of an African Renaissance thus involved not only economic and diplomatic levers, but also military levers. It was the SANDF that was employed to achieve the military objectives of the African Renaissance vision. In this spirit and using a voice from the past, the link between politics, strategy and operations is best summarised by Winston Churchill who stated "at the summit true politics and strategy are one".

This book explores the nexus of the South African National Defence Force and United Nations military conceptual models for future operations. The central theme is a strategic and operational concept for missions that is congruent between TCCs and the mission in question. A similar conceptual model for the preparation and deployment of forces will lead to a greater efficiency in the conduct of operations. Deploying forces to an international operation should require legal and moral justification.

Offensive operations in peacekeeping need to follow a similar justification to that of inter-state wars. The UNSC mandates offensive peacekeeping operations. By virtue of such a declaration, TCCs are therefore party to the conflict. The national governments of TCCs should thus make the decision of taking part in such operations with a similar seriousness to declaring limited war.

It is true that offensive operations in a UN peacekeeping setting may have more limitations than in another type of deployment. TCCs and the UN should thus have specific training and conceptual models to predict future conflict trends. The conceptual models of the UN and the respective TCCs should consequently be congruent to ensure a unity of effort.

The FIB

The creation of a peacekeeping offensive force necessitates a discussion on the law of war. The depth of such a discussion is perhaps outside of the limits of this work. However, it is a theme that requires considerable attention from the UN as a whole and TCCs in particular.

The Westphalian concept of *Jus ad Bellum* came about as a way to justify inter-state war. However, the 20th and 21st centuries have seen an increased amount of violence by non-state actors. Intra-state conflicts as well as violent acts by non-state actors have led to a wider framework for International Humanitarian Law (IHL).

The use and application of the FIB thus has to be considered within the framework of IHL. The FIB is essentially an offensive military element deployed from within a peacekeeping mission. Its status, whether as combatant or non-combatant, can thus become conflated and is consequently subject to varying opinions.

The creation and deployment of the FIB is a novel approach to the UN's use of force in peacekeeping. The FIB's aggressive strategic objectives require legal justification at a national and political level so as to strengthen the SC's mandate. The UN has justified offensive operations to neutralise certain armed groups in the DRC. The deployment of the FIB is a political tool which can further be justified in international relations by the concept of Responsibility to Protect. Regardless of justification, offensive operations make the FIB – and the MONUSCO peacekeeping mission which supports the FIB– party to the conflict. This has become a point of considerable discussion between scholars of international humanitarian law. As mentioned previously, this work will not engage the nuance of the legal argument. Nonetheless, it is important that the governments of the TCCs which comprise the FIB understand the importance of committing their forces under IHL in combat situations which are similar to war.

The UN, in short, has decided on the right to war in the DRC. This decision was largely initiated by the African regional powers in a resolve to neutralise the M23. Since the defeat of the M23, however, the performance of the FIB has been lacklustre. One should question why aggressive strategic mandate objectives on the part of the UN are met with relatively weak tactical actions.

The answer lies in the fact that the mobilisation against and defeat of the M23 was a decision made by regional African governments. This mandate was subsequently added by the UNSC to the mandate of MONUSCO. In addition to the neutralisation of the M23, the SC added various other armed groups to the MONUSCO mandate. These armed groups, including the FDLR, ADF and LRA, had a long history in the east of the DRC. They were thus not in the same way a political objective of the regional African governments or the government and Armed Forces of the Democratic Republic of the Congo (FARDC).

As they continue their offensive efforts in DRC, the Malawian, South African and Tanzanian governments are required to consider questions of *jus ad bellum* (the use of force). Where the UN has granted and justified the right to offensive operations, each government must also consider the impact of public opinion in sustaining casualties. Under its charter, the UN can authorise the use of force. UNSG Antonio Guterres has stated that the attack on the FIB in December 2017 – in which many Tanzanian soldiers were killed and injured – constitutes a war crime. This statement is subject to debate as the FIB is widely considered to be party to the conflict. The government of Tanzania must furthermore reflect on the impact of those casualties on public opinion.

South Africa has historically been sensitive to high casualties in conflict and have generally had limited casualties in their UN peace mission deployments in Burundi, DRC and Sudan. The bilateral agreement between the Central African Republic (CAR) and South Africa led to the deployment of South African troops in Bangui without a UN mandate. The deployment coincided with an uprising of Seleka rebels in 2013.This resulted in the Battle of Bangui, where approximately 30 South Africans were wounded and killed. The result was an immediate withdrawal of the SANDF from the CAR. One question, however, remains. Would South Africa be willing to experience sustained casualties in the DRC? At present there is limited evidence to suggest that South Africa would in fact be prepared to tolerate such fatalities.

The justification of the deployment of the FIB is congruent to the strategic need to stabilise sub-Saharan Africa. There is also a need to protect civilians within failed states on the continent. Although these reasons may not hold water with the public, serious consideration must be given in the continued deployment of South African forces in the FIB. In the event of extensive casualties, the South African public will most likely criticise the government. This will force the Department of International Relations and Cooperation (DIRCO) to justify the interests of South Africa in the DRC and possibly the legal and just right to 'war'.

The FIB's rules of engagement should be slightly amended to suit their aims. Their rules of engagement and that of other MONUSCO TCCs may in fact be different. The FIB's rules of engagement should be governed by very specific *jus in bello* as a result of their offensive mandate. By its nature, an offensive mandate requires the forces involved to understand and apply the principles of proportionality. The placement of the FIB within a peacekeeping mission results in the dialectic between forces with a reactionary mindset, and an FIB which requires a more proactive approach. The FIB was the result of a set of circumstances where preventative diplomacy had failed. The situation in eastern DRC was thus ripe for exploitation by rebel separatists supported by the Rwandan government.

In principle, it is widely recognised that all non-violent means should be exhausted before resorting to violent options in order to protect civilians. This in short summarises the requirement of prevention. Having declared the importance of prevention, it is also essential to understand the combat options available to support humanitarian intervention in the case where prevention results in failure.

The future deployment of peacekeeping offensive forces will most likely not take place in a pre-emptive way. The DPKO can only operate with the forces which it has available, and this is naturally governed by the national interests of TCCs.

The slow and insufficient response of the UN in Rwanda and Srebrenica in the mid-1990s are historical examples of cases that have required an aggressive response. A proportional and adequate response to such threats would have necessitated a high probability of success to be able to justify offensive action. Such a military response was ultimately dependent on the resources available and the political will and caveats of the deployed TCCs.

The difficulty lies in the balance between the political intent of a country and providing forces for UN missions to achieve strategic objectives. Within the strategic framework, and considering the limitation of resources, it is not always possible to determine whether the strategic objectives are achievable. The operationalisation of strategic objectives is thus a critical gap in the approach to peacekeeping operations. If the UNSC does not have a process to evaluate the resources and budgets required to carry out the planned mandate goals, missions become increasingly limited and flawed. The mandating of SC objectives should be defined by the resources and funds available, including the objective of neutralising of armed groups.

For offensive peacekeeping operations, an in-depth analysis should be conducted to determine what resources would be required to achieve strategic military objectives. This may include the operational strategy, concept of operations and tactics that should be employed, and the cost and resources of such operations.

The modern context for the South African military

The history of the South African military has always been inextricably linked with South African politics. The start of the 21stcentury ushered in a new terrain terms of the application of the South African military. Before 1994, the South African Defence Force was a tool of the Apartheid government. The accession to power of the ANC and the election of Nelson Mandela signified the end of the Struggle and introduced a moment of political change and the start of the new South Africa. The 21stcentury consequently saw a change in the use of the military in peacekeeping and operations other than war within the African battlespace.

The political change in South Africa was followed by a societal change which aimed at amending the unbalanced political and economic landscape. In the same way, the military went through a considerable change. The various belligerent forces operational under the Apartheid government were integrated into a brand new defence force. Two of the major players were *uMkhonto we Sizwe* (MK), the former military wing of the African National Congress (ANC) and the *Azanian People's Liberation Army* (APLA, formerly known as Poqo) – which was the armed wing of the Pan Africanist Congress (PAC). Along with non-statutory forces, the former Transkei, Bophuthatswana, Venda and Ciskei Defence Forces, MK and APLA were amalgamated with the South African Defence Force (SADF). Hence, the new South African National Defence Force (SANDF) was formed.

Naturally, the new defence force experienced teething problems with the integration. This included but was not limited to an overblown general corps, a brain drain, and a skills gap in certain services and divisions. The SANDF therefore came to represent the new South Africa in all its potential and problems. By the time the amalgamation of the SANDF was completed in the mid-to-late 1990s, the demographic and style of the South African military had been adapted to reflect a changing national and international political moment.

The new South African military became a tool of political purpose for the post-1994 government, which for the most part manifested itself in peacekeeping activities and operations other than war. Previously, the amalgamated forces of the SANDF had fought against each other and were on opposite ends of the same operational coin. The SADF had focussed on conventional and counter-insurgency operations in their attempts to suppress the ANC, APLA, and their allies. The SANDF therefore brought together forces with divergent training and operational experience, and found its existence in the African Renaissance.

As mentioned earlier, the African Renaissance was spearheaded by the former South African president Thabo Mbeki. The political moment was captured by a change of the Organisation of African Unity to the African Union. This event coincided with the launch of the New Partnership for African Development (NEPAD) and the empowerment of regional organisations.

The SANDF was deployed in the pursuit of peace and security in sub-Saharan Africa. Its deployments included crisis relief, humanitarian assistance, and peacekeeping missions in Burundi. It was also involved in the United Nations Operation in Burundi (ONUB) and in the DRC (MONUSCO). The initial focus on equatorial and eastern Africa was then extended to sub-Saharan Africa. The SANDF was deployed on a peacekeeping mission to Darfur in Sudan. That mission was the United Nations African Union Hybrid Mission in Darfur (UNAMID).

The South African military has also taken part in a number of operations on the African continent. The list includes but are not limited to Operation Boleas in Lesotho, Operation Fibre in Burundi, Operation Triton in the Comoros, Operation Amphibian in Rwanda,

Operation Montego in Liberia, Operation Cordite in Sudan, Operation Corona on the South African borders, Operation Teutonic in the DRC, Operation Mistral in the DRC, Operation Pristine in the Ivory Coast, Operation Vimbezela in the CAR, and Operation Bongane in Uganda. It has additionally participated in disaster relief missions in Mozambique and sending staff and observers to a range of missions and countries including Eritrea and Angola.

At the forefront of modern deployments is the ill-fated mission in the Central African Republic where soldiers fought at the Battle of Bangui and suffered many casualties. The mission in the CAR had politically vague and highly questionable objectives.

Considering the national priorities of the SANDF, protection of the territorial integrity of South Africa is high on the list. The SANDF is also deployed domestically in support of internal security issues related to large sporting and other international events such as the Soccer World Cup and Confederation Cup. Also included are large-scale events such as Nelson Mandela's funeral and other international conferences. The respective services, corps and divisions prepare for the required operational needs through, formal, continuous and combat readiness training and education.

Despite its involvement in significant events, there has been a fair amount of comment on the failing standards of the SANDF. There is a broad perception that the SANDF is under performing in many of its services. This may be accurate, as it is clear that many problems do exist. However, I take the view that the issue is a more nuanced one. It is true that the SANDF has been characterised by a definite loss of skills, an overblown general corps, a general state of disrepair, budgetary restrictions, problematic talent acquisition (many of those joining are doing so for employment opportunities) and the dropping of training standards. However, there have also been successes in many missions. In addition, many bright and talented soldiers, officers and generals have come to the fore. And finally, the military is for the most part not regarded as intimidating and a threat to the local population as it was seen in the pre-1994 era.

Many of the structural weaknesses of the SANDF and of the SA Army in particular, have come from political considerations and the need to reform the military to suit the post 1994 political landscape. One problematic decision has been the restructuring of divisions into Corps and Formations. This arrangement has limited the efficiency of the SA Army and SANDF and has made it challenging for them to operate as a cohesive whole.

This work does not delve into the organisational issues of the SANDF. It does, however, take a forward looking approach in terms of future conceptual models for operational application. Part of this book is also dedicated to ideas about sustainability and the development of conceptual models, theory and doctrine of the DPKO. Ultimately, the work is centred on offensive peacekeeping operations, which are currently the primary focus of South African external operations.

Chapter 1: A Conceptual Model for South African Army Future Deployment

This chapter presents a philosophical and conceptual model to determine the South African (SA) Army's approach to future operations and war. In pursuit of understanding the SA Army deployment strategy, ('how do we fight?'), this chapter suggests an experimental model comprised of two concepts. These are the SA Army Capstone Concept (SAACC) and an SA Army Future Operating Concept (SAAFOC).[1] This model is benchmarked with the concepts applied by other international armies in their determination of future operating contexts and conditions. Furthermore, the model considers the security trends present in the current strategic moment.[2]

---

[1] For the purposes of this chapter, the capstone concept refers to the overarching and guiding thought processes of the Army regarding future operations. This concept should be represented in a concept paper or document. The operating concept is subservient to the capstone concept, and addresses the way in which the army will operate in the future. The operating concept should also take the form of a concept paper. These proposed concepts should be subordinate to the Future Army Strategy. It should thus complement the Future Army Strategy, and assist to operationalise its objectives.

[2] A strategic moment is defined by M.A. Clarke as a "confluence of different trends that are at once full of possibilities, but also difficult to interpret and liable to rapidly evolve, a time when major choices with long-term consequences cannot be avoided.": UK Army,

The analysis of future security threats and trends must form the basis for the development of future SA Army capabilities and force preparation. It is within this sphere of future preparation that the chapter proposes the creation of an SAACC and operating concept. The creation of concepts and doctrine is thus designed to address the changing character of war in a complex world (US Army, 2014,p. iv).[3]

The character of war is contrasted to the nature of war which is said to be constant or at least continuous (US Army, 2014,p. 8).[4] The character of war however, remains in flux and has experienced many changes over the course of history.[5] The various military histories and

---

[3] *Joint Concept Note 2/12l Future Land Operating Concept* (Swindon: Ministry of Defence, 2012), p.iv. See SA Army Vision 2020 Team, *SA Army Strategic Profile* (Pretoria: SA Army HQ, 2006), p. i.

[4] See Australian Army, *Army's Future Land Operating Concept: Adaptive Campaigning* (Canberra: Australian Army HQ, 2009), p. iii. For a discussion on the nature of war, see, J. Angstrom, 'Introduction: Debating the Nature of Modern War', Chapter in, J. Angstrom and I. Duyvesteyn, *Rethinking the Nature of War* (New York: Frank Cass, 2005), p. 5.

[5] For information on the changing character of war, see H. Strachan and S. Scheipers (Eds), *The Changing Character of War* (Oxford: Oxford University Press, 2011); C. Holmqvist-Jonsäter and C. Coker (Eds), *The Character of War in the 21st Century* (New York: Routledge, 2010); J. Vicente, 'Toward a Holistic View of Warfare', *Empresa da Revista Militar*, 2, 3, 2009. For an interesting discussion on the character of war, refer to C.S. Gray, *War Peace and International Relations: An Introduction to Strategic History* (New

studies on the role of innovation and technology on the conduct of war illuminates the broad changing character of warfare.[6] This chapter thus proposes a conceptual system for addressing the changing character of war within the African battlespace. This system should be considered within the current South African threat perspective, which includes the possibility of conventional and unconventional operations in symmetric and asymmetric environments.[7] Current national and international thinking about

꧀꧀

York: Routledge, 2012), p. 254. For a broad view on military theories over time, see D. Coetzee and L.W. Eysturlid, *Philosophers of War: The Evolution of History's Greatest Military Thinkers Volume 1: The Ancient to Premodern World, 3000 BCE – 1815 CE* (Oxford: Praeger, 2013). For a current perspective on strategic history see H. Strachan, *Contemporary Strategy in Historical Perspective* (Cambridge: Cambridge University Press, 2013).

[6] The battle tank, manned aircraft, nuclear weapons, aircraft carrier, unmanned aerial vehicles and precision guided munitions changed the dynamics and character of war: T.G. Mahnken, *Technology and the American Way of War* (New York: Columbia University Press, 2008), pp. 222 – 224. Jeremy Black argues for the importance of technology and other societal factors which shapes and changes the character of war, J. Black, *War and Technology* (Indianapolis: Indiana University Press, 2013), p. 35.

[7] See SA Department of Defence, *South African Defence Review 2015* (Pretoria: Government Printing Works, 2015), p. 2-19. The SANDF takes a mission based approach in terms of the application of military resources. Previous threat paradigms are no longer

global security trends are similar in that they underline uncertainty and complexity in future operations (UK, 2012,p.iii).[8]

The changing character of war and the evolving future security threat forms the basis for the arguments proposed in this chapter. The SA Army deployment strategy as a broad theme of landward operational application is directly related to the anticipation of future security threats and the objectives of national strategy. The SANDF strategy determines its ends as objectives from national security policy and its ways as concepts (SANDF, 2008, p. xi). Concepts thus guide the implementation of strategic ends. The conceptual component of fighting power provides the thought processes required for the appropriate decision making and contemplation of combat.[9]

The proposed SA Army Future Deployment Strategy Concept System (SAAFDSCS) aims to understand the future deployment strategy and takes into account the importance of operations research. This research uses scientific methods to better understand military problems as per the methodology derived from the Second World War, while acknowledging its limitations (SANDF, 2010, p. 1-34).[10] The development of concepts marked a clear break from the limitations of older operations research which did not consider future changes in the conduct of war. The innovation of concepts for future warfare forms part of conceptual thinking (SANDF, 2009, pp. 4-3).

---

applicable in the SANDF: SANDF, *SANDF Military Strategy* (Pretoria: SANDF HQ, 2008), p. ix.

[8] Also see SA, *Defence Review 2015*, p. v.

[9] See SANDF, *Joint Warfare Publication 137: Defence Doctrine* (Pretoria: SANDF, 2009), p. 4-2.

[10] See C.R. Shrader, *History of Operations Research in the United States Army* (Washington: US Army, 2009).

This chapter thus finds its existence by proposing a future SAAFDSCS which includes an SAACC and an SAAFOC.

The proposed capstone concept considers the capabilities which need to be developed in consideration of future war (US Army, 2014, p. ii). The proposed operating concept is then derived from the capstone concept and addresses how the Army will operate in the future (US Army, 2014, pp.16). The SAAFDSCS will thus illuminate the requirements for future planning, resources and the development of the required forces. The findings of the capstone and operating concepts have to be considered within the overarching viewpoint of the 'Defence Review' and the SA Army Future Strategy (SAAFS). The findings and recommendations of the concepts will then have to be analysed, refined and operationalised after which it can be added into doctrine.

This chapter aims to answer the question, "how do we fight?" within the broad theme of the future SA Army force deployment strategy. This is done by suggesting the development of a future SAAFDSCS comprising an SAACC and a SAAFOC. The chapter commences with a discussion on the proposed SAACC followed by a deliberation on the proposed SAAFOC. An SAAFDSCS within the sphere of future force deployment is then proposed, and followed by a brief summary and conclusion.

Future SA Army Deployment Strategy Concept System

SA Army Capstone Concept

The SA Army Strategic Profile (SAASP) and SAAFS form a strong foundation for the conceptualisation of future conflict and the broad direction of the Army. At its core, the SAASP envisions "a professional and dynamic force" (SA Army, 2006, p. 2). A capstone concept could assist in the operationalisation of the SAAFS by conceptualising future applications and determining the direction for the development of capabilities. In making use of an international example, the United States (US) Army capstone concept speaks to the capabilities which will be required during a future period. It takes into account limited resources, hybrid threats and adaptive enemies in a complex operating environment (US Army, 2014, p. ii).

The capstone concept must compliment the SAAFS and other higher doctrinal guidance.[11]. Benchmarking with the US Army, the capstone concept should illuminate "how we think about future conflict in an uncertain and complex environment." (US Army, 2009, p.ii).

The SA Army should consider the creation of a capstone concept to strengthen and support the SAAFS project and provide a frame of reference for future operations.[12] The conceptual framework for an SAACC for landward forces should be based on current and future SA security policy challenges and realities. It should thus be based within the African battlespace while considering the dynamics of

---

[11]   The SANDF strategy is a capstone document and provides an overarching guide to the SA Army: SA, *SANDF Strategy,* p. x.

[12]   The SAACC should be founded on a Joint capstone concept. This detail, however, falls outside the scope of this chapter. The US applies a Joint capstone concept from which the other arms of service determine their capstone concepts. The Joint capstone concept is valid for 8 – 20 years: US Army War College, *How the Army Runs, A Senior Reference Handbook, 2011-2012* (Carlisle: US Army, 2011), p. 48.

uncertainty and complexity on the continent.[13] The SAACC would thus correspond with the thinking of the SA Army Landward Defence Capability Board while providing a future oriented framework. In this context, the renewal of landward defence capabilities is a strategic priority (SA, 2015, p. xi).

The capstone concept is intended to shape the way that army leaders think about future warfare (US, 2011, p. 49), and should therefore consider the factors and capabilities required in future operations. The mission success factors, superior firepower, mobility, protection and sustainment are crucial factors in the development of the SA Army (SA, 2006, p. 14). These mission success factors are fundamentally linked to the SA Army landward capabilities.

The capstone concept should amalgamate the mission success factors and the landward capabilities in terms of future conflict. The understanding of future capabilities should be enshrined in doctrine so as to provide a basis for current application. Doctrine allows knowledge on warfare to be structured and provides a common way of thinking about war (SANDF, 2006, pp. 1-2). The capstone concept should therefore be congruent to the development of current SA Army doctrine. The SAASP states that "contemporary doctrine... is awarded prime resources and is futuristically inclined to ensure a proactive instead of a reactive approach... to determine the nature of future warfare in which the SA Army will be involved" (SA, 2006,p. 12).

---

13   The scope of military threats ranges from conventional to unconventional in symmetric and asymmetric environments with the condition of complexity and the possibility of sudden escalation: SA, *Defence Review 2015*, pp. 2-19.

The development of doctrine should be accompanied by a consideration of the human and psychological aspect. In this regard, the US Army capstone concept underpins operational adaptability through flexibility and the decentralised approach (US Army, 2014, pp.ii-iii). Decentralised command is the alternative to having a centralised command structure, which is often synonymous with over control. The decentralised approach contributed to the dislocation of the German forces by maintaining a rapid decision making cycle. W.S. Lind emphasises decentralisation of command so as to ensure a decision through a rapid and efficient decision making cycle (Lind, 1985, p. 6).

The 'Defence Review' regards adaptability as a key requirement to adjust to a changing world (SA, 2015, pp. 3-13). The SA Army should hence consider a similar approach in terms of the importance of adaptability. The proposed capstone concept should include adaptability, decentralisation and mission command. All of these concepts are enshrined in SA Army and defence doctrine.[14]

The SA Army philosophy provides the broad context for complex operations in the African battlespace (SA, 2006, p. 9) The SANDF strategic concepts guides the SA Army concepts. The proposed SA Army future deployment concepts should be congruent to that of the strategic dimension. This dimension declares "rapid reaction operations for interventions, expeditionary operations to project forces for protracted periods, complex war fighting within the

---

[14]   See, SANDF, *Defence*, 4-3, SA, *SANDF Strategy*, 14-1, South African Army College, *Operational Concepts: Staff Officer's Operational Manual, Part VII* (Pretoria: 1 Military Printing Regiment, 1996), 7/6-3.

human and physical dimensions of the battle space, interoperability of command and control capabilities, and concurrency of operations in multiple theatres and joint, inter-agency, interdepartmental and multinational operations" (SA, 2015, pp. 9-10). The current international SA Army deployment focus is on peace support operations within the African battlespace.[15]

The future operations of SA Peace Support Forces as part of the United Nations Organisation Stabilisation Mission in the Democratic Republic of the Congo (MONUSCO) should be considered in the SAACC. MONUSCO is tasked to operate under Chapter VII of the UN Charter.[16]

The Force Integration Brigade (FIB) and the SA Army Engineer squadron are currently deployed in the DRC. The FIB consists of military forces from South Africa, Malawi and Tanzania. It is fundamentally an offensive force.[17] The engineer squadron is under

---

[15]   See SANDF, *Joint Warfare Publication 106: Peace Support Operations* (Pretoria: SANDF, 2009); SANDF, *Joint Warfare Publication 139: African Battlespace* (Pretoria: SANDF, 2007).

[16]   See UN Meetings Coverages and Press Releases, http://www.un.org/press/en/2016/sc12307.doc.htm, 30 March 2016. Chapter 7 of the UN Charter provides for the use of force to restore international peace in the event of a threat or breach to international peace and security: UN Charter Chapter 7, http://www.un.org/en/sections/un-charter/chapter-vii/. Retrieved 11/09/2016.

[17]   See UN Security Council Resolution 2098. The UN renewed the MONUSCO mandate and the FIB under Chapter 7 in the UN Security Council Resolution 2277: UN Meetings Coverages and Press Releases,

the tactical command of the North Kivu Brigade where the Force Engineer and Force Commander are the functional tasking authority in terms of force engineer resources.[18] The SA Army Engineers are concerned with the building of operational and non-operational infrastructure, the construction and maintenance of roads for mobility and minor explosive ordinance disposal and combat engineer tasks.[19] The FIB's role is offensive in nature and its main aim is to defeat (neutralise) rebel or armed groups in the DRC. These armed factions include the Democratic Forces for the Liberation of Rwanda (FDLR); the Allied Democratic Forces (ADF), and the

---

http://www.un.org/press/en/2016/sc12307.doc.htm, 30 March 2016. Retrieved 10/09/2016.

[18] See C.A. Dos Santos Cruz, 'Employment of Force Engineer Assets', *Interoffice Memo from MONUSCO Force Commander*, October 2015, p. 1; C.A. Dos Santos Cruz, 'Policy for Executing Engineer Works in Support of Operations', *Interoffice Memo from Force Commander*, August 2014, p. 1.

[19] See C. Prakash, 'MONUSCO Military Engineer SOP', *Force Commander MONUSCO*, November 2011, pp. 2-3; C.A. Dos Santos Cruz, 'Amendment to SOP Military Engineering', *MONUSCO Interoffice Memo from Force Commander*, July 2014, p. 1. The further application of military engineers for road building, repairs and infrastructure development is considered in post conflict reconstruction and development: T. Neethling and Heidi Hudson (Eds), *Post-Conflict Reconstruction and Development in Africa: Concepts, Role-Players, Policy and Practice* (Tokyo: UN University Press, 2013), p. 27.

Lord's Resistance Army (LRA).[20] The development of capabilities for future operations of the SA Army engineer squadron and the FIB (with support elements) should be considered in the SAACC.

The variety of peace support roles and the multiplicity of actors in the peace mission context underpin the SAASP's focus on complexity and uncertainty (SA, 2006, p. 10). An SAACC would thus direct the doctrine and Education, Training and Development (ETD) of the SA Army towards greater joint, inter-department, inter-organisational and international collaboration with other actors.[21] Furthermore, the capstone concept should consider the Army's obligation and capability development requirement in the creation of a Southern African Development Community (SADC) Standby Force[22].This should be part of the Africa Standby Force (ASF) as proposed in the Defence Review (SA, 2015, p. 7-4) and the African

---

[20]   See Mandate of MONUSCO – Security Council; UN Meetings Coverages and Press Releases, retrieved 30 March 2016 from http://www.un.org/press/en/2016/sc12307.doc.htm.

[21]   ETD should be geared towards future warfare: SA, *Defence Review 2015*, 11-12; SA, *Strategic Profile*, p. 13.
Article 4 of the AU Constitutive Act: G. Prins, 'The South African Army in its Global and Local Contexts in the early 21st Century: Mission-Critical Analysis', Chapter in, L. Le Roux, *South African Army Vision 2020 Security Challenges Shaping the Future South African Army* (Pretoria: Institute for Security Studies), p. 12.

Capacity for Immediate Response to Crises (ACIRC).[23] The ACIRC is currently a stopgap due to delays in the development and implementation of the ASF (Langille, 2015, p. 19-20). The challenges in capability development must be aimed to meet future Army needs within the regional and international security environment.

The purpose of the Army capstone concept is that it "hones the Army's understanding of emerging challenges and informs our preparation for the future, ensuring our Army stands ready to meet the demands that lie ahead." (US, 2013, p.1). The SA Army's commitment to the ASF includes a brigade tactical headquarters, a parachute infantry battalion, a motorised infantry battalion, a mortar battery, a composite engineer regiment, a tactical intelligence troop, an integrated signal squadron and a composite maintenance company (SA, 2015, pp. 7-5). The development of the capabilities required in order to execute future missions within the African battlespace requires the direction of a capstone concept.[24] This chapter thus proposes the SAACC 'operational adaptability: operations in a complex African battlespace.'[25]

---

[23]　See Anon, 'Understanding the African Standby Force, Rapid Deployment and Amani Africa II', *Institute for Security Studies Media Toolkit*, November 2015, p. 4.

[24]　The complexities of such a capstone concept have to include a multitude of operational contingencies such as the complexities of post-conflict reconstruction and development in Africa; counterinsurgency and conventional and other operations.

[25]　Higher order SANDF doctrinal guidance in the Joint Warfare Publication (JWP) series attempts to provide a baseline for understanding complex operations in the African battlespace: SANDF, *African Battlespace*, p. viii. The JWP on Peace Support Operations

The capstone concept as a 'way' of achieving national policy objectives amalgamates with the strategic objective of promoting peace, security and stability in the region and the continent (SA, 2008,p. 12). The proposed SAACC would fundamentally have to be related to an operating concept. The operating concept "describes how future Army forces, as part of joint, inter-organizational, and multinational efforts, operate" (US Army, 2014, p. 13). The second part of this chapter relates the capstone concept to the operating concept. The proposed model thus interlinks the conceptualisation of a capstone concept to the development of an operating concept.

SA Army Operating Concept

The operating concept addresses how the future Army will operate (US Army, 2014, p. 16). The future character of war is the baseline for the creation of the future operating concept (UK, 2012,pp. 1-7). The proposed SAAFOC is designed to give context and direction to the application of landward forces in the future. The idea of using an operating concept is benchmarked with international armies and their future application in the pursuit of policy objectives.[26] The operating

---

26 emphasises the importance of Peace Support Operations. The central tenets of the JWP on Peace Support Operations include the strategic context, principles, tasks and techniques and components: SANDF, *Peace Support*,pp. ix-xi.
See UK, *Future Land*; US, *Operating Concept*; Australia, *Army's Future*; US Operating Concept Summary; US, *Army Runs*, p. 49.

concept should thus be congruent to the SAAFS vision and its perception of future security threats.[27]

The Defence Review states that the international security situation is characterised by traditional and non-traditional threats including political, ethnic and regional violence. Furthermore, international terrorism, crime and cyber threats are also of great concern (UK, 2015, p. iv). The increase in complexity in the 21st century has brought on new challenges in terms of the unpredictability of threats and conflict (UK, Joint Concept, 202, pp. 1-2). The SANDF and SA Army will face operations in environments of increased human complexity which includes linguistic, ethnic, socio-economic and political dimensions. Within this context, the SANDF and SA Army will carry out non-combat and possibly major combat operations (SA, 2015, p. v).

The operating concept supplies the philosophical framework to carry out current operations. It also provides the foundation for future operations (Australia, 2009, p. i). In this context, it is of great importance for Army professionals to think about the advent of future conflict. The Army operating concept thus asks big questions about future operations which rest firmly in the relevant operating environment operate (US Army, 2014, p. iii).

The proposed SAAFOC is a means to consider the application of future landward forces in the pursuit of political objectives. The

---

[27]   See SA, *Strategic Profile*; Le Roux, *South African Army Vision 2020*; The Future SA Army Strategy project team is working on conceptualising the context of the future SA Army.

operating concept considers the importance of deterrence and the role of the use of force in achieving policy objectives.[28]

There are many factors that influence the Army operating concept and every nation state must consider its context and political objectives. The SA Army cannot apply the methods of another country's Army in the development of its own operating concept. It should rather be based on its national character and policy objectives. Much can be learnt from other national military operating concepts and theorising about future conflict.

The British operating concept considers six fundamental ideas which include understanding the battlespace, terrain, interdependence and interoperability, initiative, development of soldiers and command (UK, 2012, pp. 7-8). In philosophising about future conflict, the Australian Army considers the operational tenets of success including flexibility and agility, the adaption cycle, the human dimension and operational art (Australia, 2009, p. iv).

The US Army operating concept considers the core tenets and competencies of future conflict. The key tenets include initiative, simultaneity, depth, adaptability, endurance, lethality, mobility and innovation. The core competencies comprise shaping the security environment, setting the theatre and projecting national power. It also involves combined arms manoeuvre, wide area security, cyber space operations and special operations (US, 2014, pp. 20-23).

The SAASP considers "superior firepower, mobility, protection and sustainment capabilities that ensure a high state of readiness and ability to operate for long periods" (SA, 2006, p. 16). The operating

---

[28]   See UK, *Future Land*, p. vi; US, *Operating Concept*, p. i.

concept is intended to describe how various fighting concepts are combined (US Army, 2014, p. 31).

The SA Army Landward Defence Capability Board could determine the integration of their various capabilities in terms of future application (Interview with Senior Officer SANDF, 2016). These aspects should be considered in the proposed SAAFOC within the broader strategic goals of the SANDF.

The SANDF envisions the possibility of expeditionary campaigns and the projection and sustainment of forces in distant operating theatres (SA, 2015, p. vi). The operating concept thus considers the foundational capabilities required for future conflict without providing a definitive answer in the conduct of future war (US Army, 2014, p. 24).

The development of these capabilities are hampered by the budget limitations of the SANDF (SA, 2015: vii). Pressure to reduce defence spending is not only a South African phenomenon. Defence spending is dependent on the viewpoint of a given nation state with reference to their specific contexts.[29] The South African defence budget is 1.2% of the gross domestic product (GDP) whereas the US defence allocation is 4.9% of the GDP (SA, 2015: vii, 2-21). Despite the confines of national defence spending the SANDF is committed

---

[29]   See US, *Operating Concept*, 20–23; What are the biggest defence budgets in the world, http://www.telegraph.co.uk/news/uknews/defence/119 36179/What-are-the-biggest-defence-budgets-in-the-world.html, article retrieved 17/09/2016; Europe's Paper Militaries.
NATO Spending Still Shrinking, http://www.the-american-interest.com/2016/01/29/nato-spending-still-shrinking/. Article retrieved 17/09/2016.

to the achievement of regional security policy objectives (SA, 2015: 0-4).

The operating concept should consider the rapid deployment of land forces with minimal time spent in transition from deployment into operations. The area of operations should be anticipated to be at the end of extended Lines of Communications (LoC) in challenging conditions (US Army, 2014, p. 33). The future deployment of SA Army forces is most likely to take place in the African battlespace and under the auspices of the UN, AU or another recognised international organisation. The future deployment of such a force should be considered with respect to current trends of the development of the UN's rapid deployment capabilities (Langille, 2015, p. 4).[30]

---

[30] The AU ASF Framework Document declares that the ASF rapid deployment capability must be able to intervene in cases of genocide or imminent conflict within 14 days: Prins, 'South African Army', Chapter in, Le Roux, *Vision 2020*, pp. 12, 25. The influence of rapid deployment capabilities should also be considered doctrinally within the UN. The current UN capstone doctrine and the subordinate 1000-5000 doctrinal series should fundamentally consider the resources required for rapid reaction and rapid deployment. Furthermore, the lower level doctrine relevant to battalions should also be revised as far as rapid reaction is required. The rapid deployment concept received significant attention in the early to mid-1990s. Former UN Secretary General Boutros Boutros-Ghali advocated for peace keeping forces from all member states and rapid deployment. The failure of the UN in Somalia, Rwanda and Bosnia were indications of the limitations of peace keeping: T.

The SAAFOC for international deployments such as the FIB would have to consider rapid reaction capabilities and how to ensure that the demands of the UN are met. The resources comprise Contingent Owned Equipment (COE), and are allocated to a peacekeeping force and reimbursed. They are agreed to in the Memorandum of Understanding (MoU) between the Troop Contributing Country (TCC) and the UN.[31]

The operating concept should consider the resources and capabilities required to execute the required objectives within the framework of the mission. For example, the FIB could claim that due to the difficult and varying terrain in the DRC, the Brigade would require its own independent air assets for rapid reaction, air lift and close air support. A model for rapid tactical deployments in overcoming difficult and varying terrain can be benchmarked with the US Army during the Vietnam War which involved the use of helicopters for airlift, close support and air mobility.[32] The FIB's

Lansford (Ed), *The Political Handbook of the World* (Los Angeles: Sage, 2013), 1763. Despite previous failures, a UN rapid deployment capability is recognised by many as an effective method of conflict prevention: H.P. Langille, 'Conflict Prevention: Options for Rapid Deployment and UN Standing Forces', Chapter in, T. Wodehouse and O. Ramsbotham (Eds), *Peacekeeping and Conflict Resolution* (London: Frank Cass, 2000), p. 219.

[31] See UN DFS, Contingent Owned Equipment, http://www.un.org/en/peacekeeping/issues/fieldsupp. Accessed 13/09/2016.

[32] See C.C.S. Cheng, *Air Mobility: The Development of a Doctrine* (Westport: Praeger, 1994), 186; D.J. Mrozek,

defeat of the M23 armed group made extensive use of helicopters for airlift and air strikes and the Rooivalk was employed towards the end of the offensive.[33] The military nature of the M23 and its roots as a disgruntled faction of the DRC Army, perhaps allowed for a decisive tactical decision. Operations against the FDLR remains a challenge, not least because its members have settled in the eastern DRC and have families there, and because they continue to have political ambitions.[34] The use of military means to achieve political ends in counterinsurgency operations is multifaceted and in many ways a serious challenge.[35]

---

[33] *Air Power and the Ground War in Vietnam: Ideas and Action* (Honolulu, University Press of the Pacific, 2002), pp. 76, 77.
See S. Hoffstater, South Africa at war in the DRC – The Inside Story, 22 August 2014, http://www.timeslive.co.za/local/2014/08/22/south-africa-at-war-in-the-drc--the-inside-story. Accessed 21/9/2016.

[34] See Security Council Report, June 2016 Monthly Forecast: Democratic Republic of Congo, http://www.securitycouncilreport.org/monthly-forecast/2016-06/democratic_republic_of_the_congo_11.php. Accessed 21/9/2016.

[35] See D. Baker and E. Jordaan (Eds), *Contemporary Counterinsurgency: Roots, Practices, Prospects* (Cape Town: University of Cape Town Press, 2010), xi. See D.J. Kilcullen, *Counterinsurgency* (Oxford: Oxford University Press, 2010); P.B. Rich and I. Duyvesteyn (Eds), *Routledge Handbook of Insurgency and Counterinsurgency* (New York: Routledge, 2010).

The operating concept should thus consider the strategic objectives and the tactical realities of current and future operations. The terrain in the DRC restricts the mobility of peace keeping and enforcement forces. Air mobile forces should be considered as part of the SAAFOC jointly with the South African Air Force (SAAF). At the same time, the resource limitations of aircraft in MONUSCO and the UN should be considered.[36] This operating concept provides the context of where landward based operations are to be carried out. Terrain thus becomes a fundamental consideration (SA, 2007, p. ii).

A practical example of the context of current FIB operations is the deficiency of military engineer resources directly linked to the brigade. The tactical placement of Military Engineer Companies (MECs) under the South Kivu Brigade, North Kivu Brigade and Ituri Brigade (each of which has two MECs respectively) has limited their ability to deploy. This is exacerbated by the lack of allocated engineer resources under the direct command and control of the FIB. The FIB has an assault pioneer capability (in the form of a limited combat engineer capability) which cannot provide sufficient engineer support for the required operational tasks. These tasks often necessitate heavy machinery. The MECs of other brigades in MONUSCO are thus diverted to cater for the FIB engineer requirements which include

---

[36]   MONUSCO had 60 military helicopters in 2014: Kevin Smit Presentation, https://www.vhpa.org/heliloss.pdf. Retrieved 13/09/2016. The US military employed 12000 helicopters during the Vietnam War: Heliloss, p. 1   https://www.vhpa.org/heliloss.pdf   Retrieved 13/09/2016.

base defences and the provision of mobility.[37] The operating concept for future deployments in a rapid capacity should thus consider the lay of the land[38] and the military means for traversing rugged terrain and overcoming obstacles of physical geography.[39]

The element of physical geographical constraints as well as human complexity (ethnicity, language, religion) are fundamental considerations in future warfare. Difficult terrain may include urban areas and complex terrain, jungle, dense bush, desert, mountains and marshes.[40] These geographical terrain types may become contested

[37]   See Dos Santos Cruz, 'Engineer Works', 2. MONUSCO Military Engineer SOP, p. 1; Dos Santos Cruz, 'SOP Engineering', p. 1.

[38]   Landward operations has, is and will always be fundamentally influenced by the nature of physical terrain, UK, *Future Land*, p. 2-1.

[39]   See F.A. Galgano and E.J. Palka (Eds), *Modern Military Geography*, New York: Routledge, 2011); D.R. Caldwell, J. Ehlen and R.S. Harmon, *Studies in Military Geography and Geology* (Boston: Kluwer, 2004).

[40]   Complex terrain is defined as, "the environment shaped by physical, human and informational factors that interact in a mutually-reinforcing fashion." Australia, *Army's Future*, p. ix.
Complex terrain may include population centres, subsurface, surface and super-surface aspects in which adversaries operate, US, *Operating Concept*, p. 12. Adversaries of conventional forces are strengthened by complex terrain whereas conventional land forces seek to avoid complex terrain, UK, *Future Land*, 2-2.

battlegrounds within the African battlespace (SA, 2015, pp. 2-19).[41] A fundamental knowledge of the geographic landscape is therefore required, as is a range of requirements and capabilities for addressing these obstacles. The operating concept will thus consider, analyse and provide options in terms of the context of future operations.

In the human dimension, non-state actors present a current and future threat. Cultural knowledge is and will be of great importance, and includes an understanding of histories, customs, languages, norms and religious aspects, among others.[42] The landscape of future conflict is paved with asymmetry.[43]This may include interventions and the escalation of minor operations into major combat as well as counter-insurgency operations (SA, 2015, pp. 2-19; 2-20). The operating concept thus has to consider the capabilities required to grapple with human complexity in future operations.

The adaption of tactics in complex terrain has favoured dispersion in the view of increased lethality of modern weaponry and fires. The tactical approach of adversaries has thus adapted to individuals and or small groups with increased lethality and unpredictability. Examples of this include suicide bombers and civilian targets in city centres (Australia, 2009,p. 19). The asymmetrical edge, dispersion tactics and complex terrain are thus

---

[41]   Sun Tzu puts forward the idea of 'difficult' terrain which includes mountain forests and marshes amongst other terrain forms which are fundamentally difficult to traverse, S. Tzu, tr. A.L. Sadler, *The Art of War* (Tokyo: Tuttle, 2009), p. 69.

[42]   See SA, *Defence Review 2015*, pp. 2-19; US, *Operating Concept*, p. 18.

[43]   For further information on asymmetry in the African battlespace see SANDF, *African Battlespace*.

fundamental to the understanding of the future operating environment and should be considered in the progress of an SAAFOC.

The development of SANDF capabilities is a primary objective of the SANDF strategy (SA, 2008, p. vii). The SAAFOC proposed in this chapter is, 'winning in a complex African battlespace.' The proposed concept is congruent with the SAAFS. According to former Chief of the Army Lieutenant General Solly Shoke, the SAAFS "remains a continuous and cyclical process of revision to ensure that our thinking and activities remain relevant."[44]

Conclusion

This chapter answers the question 'how do we fight?' within the broad theme of the future SA Army force deployment strategy. In doing so, it suggests a future SAAFDCS. The proposed concept system comprises an SAACC and an SAAFOC. These concepts will determine how we will fight in future operations.

The proposed future SA Army deployment strategy concept system has been discussed and deliberated on in two sections in the chapter. The first section comprises a discussion on the SAACC which is followed by a deliberation on the proposed SAAFOC.

The SAACC must correspond and complement the SAAFS. In essence, the capstone concept should be the SA Army's guide for how to consider future conflict within the confines of uncertainty

---

[44] See S. Shoke, 'Foreword' in D. Baker and E. Jordaan (Eds), *Contemporary Counterinsurgency: Roots, Practices, Prospects* (Cape Town: University of Cape Town Press, 2010), p. ix.

and complexity. The capstone concept will direct the capability requirements which will in turn fulfil the strategic priority of renewing the landward defence capabilities. The development of a capstone concept should thus be intertwined with the Landward Defence Capability Board and its respective teams.

This chapter proposes the SAACC, 'operational adaptability: operations in a complex African battlespace.' The proposed SAACC within the future SAAFDSCS is linked to the operating concept. The operating concept should describe how a future army will operate.

The operating concept addresses how an army will fight with the advent of complex terrain and human complexity in the African battlespace. The SAAFOC proposed in this chapter is, 'winning in a complex African battlespace.'

This chapter finds its existence at the nexus between the continuities of the nature of war and the constant change in the character of war. The changing character of war questions the shape and form of the SA Army as well as the capabilities required for future operations. It is within this vein that the chapter considers the required future SAAFDSCS for the planning and understanding of future war.

The suggested concepts should be limited by their forward projection. Due to the continuous change in the operational landscape, these notions must exist in fluidity. The capstone concept and operating concept can be created for current operation with a future view of five to eight years or the corresponding amount of years as is practicable.

The solution to the question 'how do we fight?' is thus answered through presenting a philosophical model, and not a prescriptive method for future SA Army operations. The proposed SAAFDSCS is benchmarked with international armies. Furthermore, the proposed system is conceptual and outlines the process of determining how we will fight in the future. It requires further development into substantive concept chapters which exceeds the scope of this chapter.

The proposed SAAFDSCS will determine the capabilities required in conjunction with the Landward Defence Capability Board. The operating concept will help in the understanding of how we will fight in the future. The concept system could thus facilitate the SA Army future vision and assist in the philosophical and practical preparations for future operations.

Chapter 2: United Nations Offensive Peacekeeping Operations: Theory and Doctrine

The strategic decision of the UN to pursue offensive operations in order to achieve mandate objectives in peacekeeping missions was met with a mixed response by the international community.[45] Many observers regard the decision of deploying the FIB in MONUSCO – and the mandating of unilateral offensive operations in peacekeeping – to be contradictory to the principles of impartiality and non-use of force except in self-defence and defence of the mandate. The fact that the UN, in response to certain threats, has opted for the use of combat

---

[45] See P. Cammaert, "The UN Intervention Brigade in the Democratic Republic of the Congo", *International Peace Institute*, 2013; E. P. Rhoads, "Perils of Peacekeeping without Politics", *Rift Valley Institute,* 2013;S. Sheeran and S. Case, "The Intervention Brigade: Legal Issues for the UN in the Democratic Republic of the Congo", *International Peace Institute*, 2014; M. Berdal and D.H. Ucko, 'The Use of Force in UN Peacekeeping Operations', *The Rusi Journal Article*, 160, p. 1, 2015; J. Stearns, "Can Force be Useful in the Absence of a Political Strategy? Lessons from the UN missions to the DR Congo", *Global Peace Operations Review*, 2015; E.H. Rhoads, *Taking Sides in Peacekeeping: Impartiality and the United* Nations (Oxford: Oxford University Press, 2016); C. De Coning, "Peace Enforcement in Africa: Doctrinal Distinctions between the African Union and United Nations", *Contemporary*, 38, p. 1, 2017.

operations necessitates a new way of thinking about peacekeeping operations.

The point of departure of this chapter, is that the UN has until present not defined offensive operations, and specified what this means in practice. There is therefore a need for the UN to describe the exact nature of offensive operations. This should occur across the levels of peacekeeping so as to be clear as to what it entails.

Furthermore, several questions also need to be asked. Are offensive operations restricted to tactical level mobile ground operations with limited indirect fire and attack helicopter/gunship support (robust peacekeeping)? How do strategic mandates regarding offensive operations influence peacekeeping doctrine? Should there be an organisational doctrine that guides the military strategic concept of operations (CONOPS)? Do offensive operations only encompass conventional operations or do they include counterinsurgency? Once there is a clear understanding of what offensive operations entail, doctrinal guidance for the strategic, operational and tactical levels of peacekeeping should be created. This is currently a gap which may result in less than optimal efficiency in operations.[46]

The aim of this chapter is to propose a UN military strategic and operational framework for the conduct of efficient offensive

---

[46] For research which goes beyond UN offensive operations see C. De Coning, C. Aoi and J. Karlsrud, Peacekeeping in a New Era: Adapting to Stabilization Protection and New Threats. New York: Routledge. This work indicates gaps in the political and strategic UN peacekeeping doctrine and provides an in depth study on the topic

operations in peacekeeping. The military strategic and operational framework suggested in this study is motivated by the MONUSCO Security Council (SC) Resolutions, 2098 (2013) through to 2348 (2017), which urges that MONUSCO improve its operational effectiveness through lessons learned (UN, 2017, p. 15). Two main proposals regarding offensive operations find their origin in the aim of this chapter. They include suggestions on:

- amendments to doctrine regarding offensive operations across the level of peacekeeping,
- theoretical constructs regarding offensive operation (manoeuvre theory).

This chapter acknowledges the evolution of modern peacekeeping from its traditional model into multidimensional complex peacekeeping. Since 2013, the unilateral use of force to neutralise Armed Groups in the DRC has been included in the lexicon of UN peacekeeping mandates (FIB).This incorporation has added a new dimension to the already multifaceted phenomenon of complex peacekeeping. Although the use of force on the tactical level was not entirely new, the strategically mandated independent use of force added a new layer of complexity to the SC's strategic intent in relation to the conflict in the DRC.[47]

From a strategic military perspective, the Principles and Guidelines of UN Peacekeeping Operations (Capstone Doctrine) make no

---

[47] See Security Council Resolutions, 2293 (2016), 2277 (2016), 2211 (2015), 2198 (2015), 2147 (2014), 2136 (2014), and 2098 (2013).

provision for the strategic and operational guidance for offensive operations. The use of force in the Capstone Doctrine is directed to influence military spoilers and 'not seek their defeat' (UN DPKO/DFS, 2008,p. 35). It must be recognised that the UN has published an official guideline on the use of force, entitled, "Use of Force by Military Components in United Nations Peacekeeping Operations". This publication, however, marks a departure from the Capstone doctrinal guidance on the use of force in terms of the neutralisation of Armed Groups. Furthermore, where the abovementioned guideline indicates that the objective of offensive operations is to neutralise Armed Groups, it only refers to the Mandate and Rules of Engagement, as guiding documents for the execution of operations. No reference is made to the mission concept or to CONOPS (UN, 2017, p. 24). Moreover, significant gaps in UN doctrine for independent offensive operations remain.

The decision to mandate offensive combat operations under the banner of the DPKO should not be taken lightly. Such operations pose inherent difficulties on the tactical level with multi-cultural and polyglot forces. It may also set a challenging precedent on the political level, whether formally or tacitly.

The UN's decision to use offensive operations should be based on a firm theoretical construct. The conduct of operations should be grounded in military tradition. UN forces, recruited from across a range of military systems have, however, varying competing and occasionally complimentary doctrinal customs. In order to limit the confusion of diverging doctrinal backgrounds, this chapter suggests the use of manoeuvre theory as a basic construct in which to frame UN offensive operations and the creation of UN joint doctrine for offensive operations. This recommendation should complement the planning process involving SC Resolutions, Integrated Strategic

Frameworks, Military Capability Studies, Mission Concepts, CONOPS and Operational Orders.

The understanding of combat operations is of great importance. This chapter responds to the recommendation by the High-Level Independent Panel on United Nations Peace Operations (HIPPO) report. It was advocated that the UN secretariat become more field focussed (HIPPO, 2015, p. viii), in that offensive operations be studied and understood by the UN headquarters.[48]

UN Strategic Mandate for Neutralising Armed Groups: Towards a doctrine for Offensive Operations

By framing operations within a theory of war, the construct will assist commanders in the way that they think about operations and the way in which they state their intent. It will further promote confidence in the military decision making cycle. Doctrine is a reflection of institutionalised knowledge and provides direction on 'how' to carry out operations, where theory provides a broad view and understanding of offensive operations (Angstrom& Widen, 2015, p. 5).

This section proposes that a UN doctrine be created which defines offensive operations. This particular doctrine would be required to address how a force fights across the various levels of peacekeeping. The main function of doctrine is that while it defines institutional methods about what works in combat; it also indicates

---

[48] The chapter acknowledges that the HIPPO report suggests caution in the conduct of UN offensive operations (HIPPO, 2015,p. x).

institutional values and the way that people talk and think about military missions (Hoiback, 2013, pp. 116-120).

The book 'UN Peacekeeping Doctrine in a New Era: Stabilization, Protection and New Threats', is a seminal work on contemporary UN doctrine. The work examines the gap between UN peace operations as a whole and the lack of available doctrinal guidance. Focusing on political, strategic and national doctrines, the book proposes new typologies for UN peacekeeping doctrine (De Coning, Aoi& Karlsrud, 2017). Offensive operations in the DRC marks a departure from traditional peace enforcement doctrine. This precept is defined as military force used at the strategic or operational level, without the consent of the main parties, or where a political process is absent or difficult to attain and where there is harm to civilians (UN DPKO/DFS, 2008,p. 42).

The UN has claimed that its operations in the DRC do not constitute peace enforcement (De Coning, 2017, p. 154). This chapter builds on the idea that the UN requires an amendment in doctrine and focusses on the doctrinal adjustments as relevant to the application of offensive operations. The change in operational need and doctrine is necessitated by evolving international security threats.

The change in the character of conflict has necessitated changes in the UN's approach to peacekeeping. This has included a renewed focus on offensive operations such as the creation of the FIB in the DRC. Moreover, there have been more robust offensive inclined operations in Mali (against violent extremists utilising improvised explosive devices) and in the CAR. The UN decision to make use of offensive forces was a result of the strategic moment in which it found itself. M.A. Clarke defines a strategic moment as a "confluence of different trends that are at once full of possibilities, but also difficult to interpret and liable to rapidly evolve, a time when major

3

choices with long-term consequences cannot be avoided." (UK Army, 2012, p.iv). The strategic moment of the UN is the result of the progression of violent trends over the last few years and the UN's concomitant response.

During the early 1990s, the UN was hopeful to reaffirm the envisioned peace of the historic UN Charter. The post-Cold War security environment was viewed enthusiastically with aspirations of establishing a broad peace through traditional, Chapter VI, buffer force peacekeeping operations. The failures in Rwanda, Yugoslavia and Somalia, however, provided a heavy and sobering blow to traditional peacekeeping models indicating their profound limitations.

Multidimensional peacekeeping developed from traditional peacekeeping in response to the growing complexity of conflicts where often there was no peace to keep. The role of civilian peacekeepers became more prominent. This was a direct result of the need to address human rights violations, monitoring of elections, setting up of transitional administrations and provision of humanitarian assistance among other broad requirements. These matters reached beyond the scope of the military, which meant that civilian peacekeepers were also required.[49] Multidimensional peacekeeping should be guided by the supremacy of the political process in conflict affected countries, and draws its strength from the

---

[49]   See UN DPKO, *Handbook on United Nations Multi-Dimensional Peacekeeping Operations* (New York: UN, 2003); M.W. Doyle and N. Sambanis, *Making War and Building Peace: United Nations Peace Operations* (Princeton: Princeton University Press, 2006); DPKO/DFS, *Peacekeeping Operations Principles and Guidelines (Capstone Doctrine)*, 2008.

political will of states supporting the UN, as highlighted in the *Brahimi* and HIPPO Reports.

Within the sphere of politico-strategic intent, the UN mandated the use of offensive operations in neutralising Armed Groups in the Democratic Republic of the Congo (SC, 2017,p. 11).[50] From a strategic viewpoint, this indicates the resolve and intent of the SC. The strategic-operational-tactical question which results from the decision is: how does one define the use of force in offensive operations? If the UN considers offensive operations limited to conventional mobile attacks, then the question is posed as to whether such offensives are sufficient to defeat politically motivated Armed Groups.

The HIPPO report advises caution in the use of offensive operations in peacekeeping missions (HIPPO, 2015, p. x). Many modern commentators hold similar opinions on the unguided use of force in peace missions (Blyth &Cammaert, 2016). The use of force in peace missions versus the political will and interests of TCCs remain a hot topic for political debate. At the same time, on a practical level, UN headquarters and field personnel require a guiding framework for the execution of offensive operations. The application of offensive operations should support the nature, principles and objectives of the UN. SC Resolution 2348 (based on SC Resolution 2098 (2013) and subsequent resolutions) called for highly mobile robust operations to neutralise Armed Groups in the DRC (SC, 2017, p. 11).

---

[50] See Security Council Resolutions, 2293 (2016), 2277 (2016), 2211 (2015), 2198 (2015), 2147 (2014), 2136 (2014), and 2098 (2013).

The FIB was created in 2012 as a result of MONUSCO's ineffective tactical response to the M23 rebel group in that same year. The FIB was formed by regional actors who had the political will to take decisive steps to put down the M23 rebellion. The AU and Southern African Development Community (SADC)[51] however lacked the security infrastructure and economic means to facilitate an independent mission in the DRC. As a result, the FIB was deployed under the banner of the UN.

A fundamental disconnect is noted in a study of the strategic and tactical relationship which resulted from MONUSCO's inability to respond to the M23 rebellion prior to the establishment of the FIB. The Chapter VII mandate was sufficient to authorise the use of force for the protection of the mandate and to defend Goma against the M23. Furthermore, robust peacekeeping has been used on various previous occasions in the DRC.[52] Nonetheless, the combination of the risk appetite of the respective Force and contingent commanders as well as the political will of the TCCs were factors in MONUSCO's inability to defend Goma against M23 rebels. The outcome was a strategic blunder in that the mandate was not fulfilled through the lack of ability or will on the tactical level. As a result, the decision was taken at the strategic level to reinforce the objectives of security

---

[51]   The HIPPO report acknowledges the importance of global-regional partners in promoting international peace and security and the importance of the UN in facilitating the strategic vision of such partnerships (HIPPO, 2015: pp. XI, XII).

[52]   See P. Cammaert, "The UN Intervention Brigade in the Democratic Republic of the Congo", *International Peace Institute*, 2013.

through explicitly developing the mandate of offensive operations to neutralise Armed Groups.

The decision of the UN to consider offensive military operations as a strategic means requires a framework for execution. The chapter recognises the UN's planning and execution methods. These procedures include but are not limited to Integrated Strategic Frameworks, Mission Concepts, Military Capability Studies, CONOPS and Operational Orders. The strategic framework for execution is by its nature multifaceted and challenging, given the confluence of diverging actors and threats. It stands to reason that offensive operations are proportionally more challenging with the increased complexity of Armed Groups, context and terrain.

To cite examples from current missions where the security situation involves asymmetric, guerrilla warfare threats from non-state actors, such as Mali and the CAR, the UN should carefully consider its strategic options in terms of the use of robust peacekeeping and offensive operations. The creation of a guiding joint doctrine for offensive operations across the levels of peacekeeping will address the strategic-operational-tactical relationship between the UN, regional partners and TCCs. It will also render operations more efficient and interoperable.

Furthermore, such doctrine will guide the supply of forces, the execution of operations and the processing of intelligence. This is particularly important in the case of Mali. Even though the mission does not have a strategic mandate for offensive operations, the host of actors in the area of operations complicates operational efficiency. This impediment is the result of the G5 Sahel, Barkane and UN forces operating under divergent doctrines. In the process of creating a new doctrine, the UN will be required to define the limits of offensive operations and neutralisation of Armed Groups in peacekeeping.

Offensive operations are defined by the US Field Manual 3-0 Operations, as the "operations [that] aim to destroy or defeat an enemy...and achieve decisive victory" (US Army, 2001). Does the neutralisation of Armed Groups in the DRC refer to the decisive defeat of such groups? By defining offensive operations, the UN will promote understanding and clarity. The formation of clear doctrine throughout all levels of peacekeeping including definitions, force and organisational command relationships, will further promote efficiency and interoperability.

The execution of military operations remains subjective to interpretation. The tactics of each state are also dependent on their particular national doctrine. The use of a common military strategic framework, on the operational and strategic levels, will assist with interoperability between polyglot TCCs with often diverging military traditions. It will, however, respect the TTPs of the individual states.

This chapter suggests that the UN should frame its combat operations within a particular theory of war. This theory should be clearly stated in the Capstone Doctrine and the various military manuals. These should include but not be limited to the Infantry Battalion Manual, Military Engineer Manual and Special Forces Manual. The aforesaid manuals set out[53] the traditional roles of

---

[53] See UN, 'UN Infantry Battalion Manual', DPKO/DFS, 2012; UN, 'UN Peace Missions Military Engineer Unit Manual', DPKO/DFS, 2015; UN, 'UN Peace Missions Military Reconnaissance Unit Manual', DPKO/DFS, 2015; UN DPKO//DFS, 'Aviation Manual', 2005. In terms of intelligence doctrine,see O. Abilova and A. Novosseloff, "Demystifying Intelligence in UN Peace

Infantry, Engineers, Special Forces, and Air Support, among other force elements.

As an example, the UN Infantry Battalion Manual states that the UN peacekeeping battalion does not manoeuvre in offensive and defensive operations (UN DPKO/DFS, 2012, p. 86). An addition therefore needs to be made to address more offensive roles envisioned and mandated by the UN. The Mission Concept, CONOPS and Operational Orders must be similar for all parts of a given mission and in the case of MONUSCO, the framework forces and FIB must have the same objectives and guiding instructions to ensure efficiency and interoperability.

By declaring the military theory and conceptual direction of offensive operations, the UN will promote clarity among civilian and military peacekeepers and between the strategic, operational and tactical levels. This should in turn be reflected in doctrinal guidance across the levels of peacekeeping. The Capstone Doctrine, or relevant doctrinal documents or addenda outlining offensive operations, will assist in informing the strategic and operational concepts of campaigns and combat operations. These strategic and operational concepts should be tied to a clear intelligence picture on the various levels of peacekeeping.[54] The focus should be rapid high impact and highly mobile operations which secures strategic results.

Operations: Toward an Organizational Doctrine", *International Peace Institute*, 2016; UN DPKO/DFS, 'Policy: Peacekeeping Intelligence', 2017.

[54] See UN DPKO/DFS, 'Policy: Peacekeeping Intelligence', 2017.

The victory of the FIB over the M23 has indicated the ability of tactical actions to succeed against rebel groups in UN peacekeeping operations.[55] The use of small, well trained fighting forces with a background in manoeuvre warfare doctrine has also succeeded. This has occurred outside of the ambit of UN peacekeeping operations in conducting efficient functions with strategic success in Africa. An example of this is the operations of Executive Outcomes in Sierra Leone (Barlow, 2015).

The implementation of a UN military strategic framework and manoeuvre theory through an offensive peacekeeping doctrine does not discount attrition theory, nor does it guarantee victory and the attainment of political solutions. It does, however, provide the best systematic method for the achievement of political objectives through the use of military means. The military strategic framework[56] for offensive operations can be developed from the UN's existing tools. These mechanisms include the Integrated Strategic Framework, Mission Concept and CONOPS. All three are designed to implement strategic mandate objectives through operationalisation of plans and

---

[55] The victory over M23 was also successful because of regional political pressures exerted on Rwanda, which, as a supporter of rebels in the east of the Democratic Republic of the Congo, was widely regarded as a spoiler. See J. Stearns, "Can Force be Useful in the Absence of a Political Strategy? Lessons from the UN missions to the DR Congo", *Congo Research Group*, 2015.

[56] See J.R. Cerami and J.F. Holcomb, *US Army War College: Guide to Strategy* (Carlisle: Strategic Studies Institute, 2001).

tactical execution.[57] The tactical level execution of offensive operations is central to achieving strategic goals. It is evident that neither sphere can exist in isolation.

In order for a military victory to be translated into political capital, an opposing force must be defeated and ground must be captured and defended. Where UN manpower is insufficient in holding terrain, national and allied forces should be used. When a military victory is not followed up by the placement of conventional forces in the conquered area, a power vacuum will most likely be created. This will result in the replacement of the old rebel forces with new ones.[58] The limited success of the Armed Forces of the Democratic Republic of the Congo (FARDC) in consolidating FIB gains must be questioned (Cammaert, 2013, p. 1). The strategies of the UN and the host state must thus share a similar vision. UN doctrinal guidance should refer to how to execute offensive

---

[57] See UN Integrated Strategic Framework; Mission Concept; Multi-year strategies for UN Agencies; UN, *Planning Toolkit*, 2012; The Concept of Operations (CONOPS) is developed with TCCs at the start of a mission and in accordance with the modification of mandate objectives.

[58] In a case where rapid offensive forces are used to secure objectives, upon the defeat of the opposing force, an additional conventional force must be placed on the ground to secure and dominate the area. This could be forces of the state being assisted or conventional Chapter VI peacekeeping forces. It should be noted that Chapter VI forces will most likely be regarded as party to the conflict because of their association with the offensive force.

operations and how to gain operational and politico-strategic objectives from tactical execution.

The FIB's tactical defeat of the M23 gave hope to UN offensive operations. Even so, political dealings and accomplishments following the victory remain debatable. The FIB subsequently achieved limited success against the Democratic Forces for the Liberation of Rwanda (FDLR). The FDLR have political objectives and their members have become immersed in the local community within eastern DRC. In this case, conventional operations may not be sufficient. Rather, a counterinsurgency strategy may be required in the event that an offensive approach be further pursued (Garcia, 2017, p. 9).[59]

In 2005, Major General Patrick Cammaert utilised a strategy against the FDLR which bore similarities to counterinsurgency operations (Baker &Jordaan, 2010, p. 157). In the event of intervening in insurgency or in contexts where the local population is hostile towards the UN, a counterinsurgency strategy could be considered to complement combat operations. This is of course subject to the mandate, political climate and international interest within the SC.

These military and political considerations go beyond the scope of this chapter, and the complexity in the study of strategy is subject to the context of the mission in question. The national political considerations of TCCs, which are averse to risk, may make

---

[59]   See D. Baker and E. Jordaan (Eds), *Contemporary Counterinsurgency: Roots, Practices, Prospects* (Cape Town: University of Cape Town Press, 2010); US Army, *Field Manual 3-24.2 Tactics in Counterinsurgency* (Washington, US Army, 2009).

counterinsurgency operations unlikely. While this chapter does not express an opinion about the use or implementation of counterinsurgency operations and strategies in peacekeeping missions, they may be a natural consideration as a result of the progression of combat operations.

The defeat of guerrilla, unconventional or insurgent forces has been studied in depth by military and political scientists and theorists, and the overwhelming conclusion is that it is a fundamentally herculean and problematic project to undertake for national or coalition militaries. Jim Terrie states that it is doubtful as to whether UN peacekeeping forces would be able to apply a counterinsurgency strategy due to capability restrictions and low troop levels (Baker &Jordaan, 2010, p. 152).

Neutralising Armed Groups has non-military consequences which may require civilian peacekeeping and UN police involvement. Following the defeat of Armed Groups, the civilian peacekeeping component has an important role to play in political advocacy, community liaison and monitoring and evaluation following the termination of hostilities. Furthermore, in the event of the defeat of Armed Groups in the DRC, an appropriate UN, MONUSCO, and DRC police plan of action is required. Such a strategy will mitigate the potential effect of rebels/insurgents in local villages. Offensive operations doctrine should be holistic and should ensure that community liaison assistants, police and other UN tools are effectively used and integrated.

UN doctrine for offensive operations should thus address the limits and definitions of offensive operations when strategically mandated. The doctrine should build on the UN guideline on the use of force (2017). It should moreover extend across the strategic, operational and tactical levels of peacekeeping so as to ensure an

3

effective and holistic understanding of the topic. Furthermore, such a doctrine should highlight interoperability with other regional partners such as the North Atlantic Treaty Organisation (NATO) and the AU.[60] Where manoeuvre theory provides a construct for the conduct of operations, doctrine should guide the execution of operations without being overly prescriptive (US, 2014, p. 70). Doctrine provides the *how to* in operations where concepts look to the future of peacekeeping.

---

[60]   See C. De Coning, "Peace Enforcement in Africa: Doctrinal Distinctions between the African Union and United Nations", *Contemporary*, 38, 1, 2017.

Chapter 3: Manoeuvre Theory: A Proposed Framework for UN Offensive Operations on the Strategic and Operational Levels of Peacekeeping

The study of war is broad and multifaceted and military staff and defence colleges dedicate extended periods to the study of this phenomenon. Whereas war fighting and peacekeeping are not synonymous, there are certainly some elements of war fighting that overlap with peacekeeping. Among them are robust peacekeeping, peace enforcement and offensive operations. In the study of war, there are two main theories: manoeuvre and attrition. These two broad overarching frameworks influence the commander's thinking about war and the ways in which operations are executed. The theories are not mutually exclusive and operations and wars often combine the two constructs on different occasions and on the different levels of war (Springman 2006, p. 1).

By choosing offensive operations, the UN may have to publish a doctrine on its combat operations which should generally be framed in a theory of war. Manoeuvre warfare theory, although based largely on Cold War conventional warfare theory, is a construct that can be applied to limited forces in small operations as well as to large forces in high intensity operations. In terms of modern history, there are a number of prominent examples which support manoeuvre theory. Three of these instances are briefly described next.

Firstly, following the First Gulf War, NATO adopted manoeuvre warfare as its tactical doctrine. Secondly, the attrition focused Vietnam War led the United States of America (USA) to re-analyse its approach to warfare resulting in a focus on manoeuvre theory. And finally, Africa has had its own unique experience in warfare where manoeuvre theory with limited forces has demonstrated great value.[61]

With regard to tactical doctrine, tactics, techniques and procedures are left to the authority of TCCs (UN DPKO, 2008, p. 9). The UN has the authority and responsibility to frame the tactical means within a theoretical construct of offensive operations applied within the broader operational and strategic levels of peacekeeping.

---

[61] See H. Frantzen, *NATO and Peace Support Operations 1991-1999: Policies and Doctrines* (London: Frank Cass, 2005); US Field Manual (FM) 100-5; US Marine Field Manual, FMFM 1-5; E. Barlow, Barlow, *Composite Warfare: The Conduct of Successful Ground ForcesOperations in Africa* (Solihull: Helion, 2015); M. Kainerugaba, *Battles of the Ugandan Resistance A Tradition of Maneuver* (Kampala: Fountain, 2010); S. Fitzsimmons, *Mercenaries in Asymmetric Conflict* (Cambridge: Cambridge University Press, 2013); R. De Vries, *Mobiele oorlogvoering: 'n perspektief vir Suider-Afrika* (Pretoria: Harman, 1987); R. De Vries, *Eye of the Firestorm: Strength Lies in Mobility* (Johannesburg: Naledi, 2013); E. Jordaan, 'An Airborne Capability from South Africafrom a Special Operations Forces Perspective', *Scientia Militaria*, 40, 1, 2012; F. Vrey, A. Esterhuyse, and T. Mandrup, *On Military Culture: Theory, Practice and African Armed Forces* (Cape Town: University of Cape Town, 2014); A. Garcia, 'A Manoeuvre Warfare Analysis of South Africa's 1914-1915 German South West African Campaign' *Scientia Militaria*. 45, 1, 2017.

Manoeuvre warfare attempts to gain victory through focussing on the operational level of war, and wherever possible, avoiding unnecessary pitched battles. Within the framework of manoeuvre theory, the role of the commander is to defeat the enemy and not necessarily destroy the enemy (Leonhard 1994, pp. 24-29). The alternative theory to manoeuvre is attrition theory. Where manoeuvre warfare emphasises the human element of war, attrition theory has a distinct focus on the technological aspect of war and the destruction of the enemy's mass (Leonhard 1994,p. 19). Theorists must concede that technological developments have fundamentally changed the shape of warfare on tactical and operational levels. The need for military theory, however, remains a constant for military practitioners, historians, analysts and strategists alike.

In the conduct of operations, there will ordinarily be a relationship and continuum between attrition and manoeuvre warfare theory. Manoeuvre theory in its purest form may not always be attainable. This is because it is a rapid victory with minimal loss of life. Nonetheless, it provides an ideal to be strived for and a better option than attrition.

There are three main methods of achieving victory through manoeuvre warfare theory: pre-emption, disruption and dislocation. Pre-emption is the use of manoeuvre in aprophylactic way to prevent the outbreak of combat (Simpkin 1986, p. 140). There are historical examples of successful pre-emptive tactical offensive operations in the DRC. These were executed under Chapter VII mandates (Blyth & Cammaert, 2016).

Adding to the discussion on pre-emption, the Under Secretary-General (USG) for Peacekeeping Operations, stated that operations would include, "adapting our capabilities and our field support to allow Missions to act in an agile, mobile, robust and pre-emptive manner" (Ladsous, 2015). This method may be achievable with a rapidly deployable UN force. It may also be brought about successfully where a force is in theatre, and is rapidly transferred to another area where a flare-up of violence may occur. The manual provides a guide for the time-spans for the redeployment of UN Infantry Battalions. It indicates that an Infantry Battalion Quick Reaction Force (company group) should be deployable anywhere in the Battalion area of operations within two hours, anywhere within the Mission area of operations in six hours and inter-mission within twenty four hours (UN DPKO/DFS, 2012, p. 72).

Dislocation and disruption are the other means of achieving victory through manoeuvre warfare which occur after the conflict has commenced. These means of achieving victory can be adopted and incorporated into the relevant UN doctrinal documents so as to shape the way we think about offensive military operations.

Pre-emption is preventative and makes use of speed, (British Army 2010, pp. 5-16; Leonhard 1994, pp. 63-64), dislocation and disruption. This occurs after the outbreak of violence, and involves attacking the centre of gravity and the physical and psychological spheres of the enemy, epitomising surprise while avoiding the enemy strengths and attacking weak points (South African Army College 1996, pp. 7/5-6; British Army 2010,pp. 5-16). Carl von Clausewitz coined the term, 'centre of gravity.' This refers to the hub of all power, on which victory depends (Von Clausewitz, 2006, p. 119). Manoeuvre theory modified the concept of centre of gravity and redefined it as 'critical vulnerability'. When one is attacked, critical vulnerability would lead to the defeat of the enemy through paralysis (Leonhard, 1994,p. 44).

The military strategic framework verifies the importance of manoeuvre warfare (Gooch 1996; Baylis 1987; Van Creveld 1991;

Handel 1992; Olsen and Gray 2011; Gray 2007). The framework also links political interests, the use of the military and the different levels of war/peacekeeping. The levels of war/peacekeeping provide the framework to understand the process of planning and applying Chapter VI, Chapter VII and unilateral offensive operations. This planning and application is executed in order to achieve strategic objectives.

Between the strategic level of war/peacekeeping and the tactical level of war/peacekeeping, there is the operational level of war/peacekeeping. The operational level traditionally refers to the conduct of campaigns. The tactical level refers to battles (Leonhard 1994,p. 9). In peacekeeping, the tactical level may also include the efforts of civilian peacekeepers. Where the TCCs can determine the use of TTPs, the UN can provide the theoretical framework at the strategic and operational levels for the conduct of the campaign. Campaigns are fought at the operational level of war, which links the strategic objectives to military actions at the tactical level. When analysing the levels of war versus the levels of peacekeeping, one has to deliberate on the limitations and considerations specific to the UN.

Fundamentally, the levels of war include the strategic, operational and tactical levels. The respective level of war dictates the type of military planning and action that is required. This process must be mimicked for UN offensive operations. The strategic level concerns itself with objectives and mandates as set out by the SC. The contribution of military forces by TCCs are also of strategic concern and their national political interests influence the quantity and type of forces deployed. The operational level pertains to mission headquarters and campaigns and is organised around force and mission leadership. The tactical level refers to battles and engagements – usually with divisions, brigades and battalions. The tactical level also provides the setting where civilian peacekeepers carry out critical tasks for the mission.

The commitment of UN forces in peace operations may be smaller than the military forces deployed in conventional wars.However, the planning process and the conceptual model for campaigns and battles remain similar. The execution of military and civilian actions on the tactical level must theoretically translate to the achievement of strategic objectives.[62] Figure 1 shows the levels of peacekeeping and the UN guiding documentation.

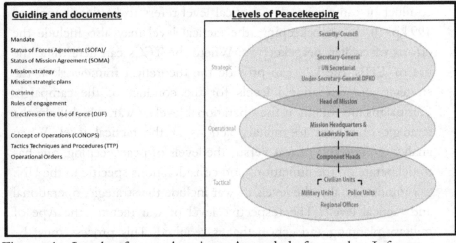

Figure 1: Level of peacekeeping. Amended from the Infantry Battalion Manual (UN DPKO/DFS, 2012, p. 55)

---

[62] In this regard certain strategic objectives cannot be operationalised.

Each level of war has its respective centre of gravity and thus its critical vulnerability. It is therefore suggested that prior to undertaking offensive operations, the UN determine the centre of gravity of the opposing force (Mission Concept/CONOPS) and then execute the required operations using a combat doctrine and military theory. The operational level is where the political and strategic objectives are realised and it is where manoeuvre warfare is executed. The operational level of war/peacekeeping is controlled by the UN where the tactical level is subject to the TTPs of the respective TCCs. Should the UN not wish to be in command on the strategic and operational levels – or if the reality of tactical operations result in the respective home governments of TCCs in making distance operational decisions in the mission area – then it could be that offensive operations should be avoided as a means to achieve SC strategic objectives in peacekeeping.

The efficiency of missions relies on the command structure. In terms of traditional military headquarters and structure, the command structure is non-existent on the strategic level of the UN. Where the strategic level has its inherent difficulties, the appointment of the correct military commanders for the required combat centred missions would greatly improve tactical efficiency. This should be done as soon as possible and where feasible during the initiation or planning phase (CONOPS). In practical terms, the CONOPS should clearly identify centres of gravity in conjunction with TCCs. The focus should not only be on the quantities of uniformed personnel required but the CONOPS should be guided by an overarching doctrine and military theory so as to define offensive operations, neutralising of Armed Groups and the ways and means required.

The concept of achieving victory with minimal loss is central to manoeuvre theory. The SC Resolution 2348 states that Armed

Groups in the DRC should be neutralised by offensive operations which should be conducted "in a robust, highly mobile and versatile manner" (UN, 2017, p. 11). The main reason for the compatibility of manoeuvre warfare with the UN offensive operation mandates is the general aversion of TCCs to high risk, attrition and losses. The use of pre-emption makes use of mobility, speed and surprise –rather than firepower – to achieve its objective. In making use of minimal direct fire engagements, it reduces the risk of casualties (Leonhard 1994 p. 64). The use of minimal force appeals to the UN. The low intensity firepower/highly mobile operations will most likely have to be combined with air support and engineering capabilities.

Offensive operations may be limited in cases where Armed Groups have some amount of strategic depth, as afforded by support bases across national borders. Examples include Chad-Darfur Sudan and DRC-Uganda among others. Offensive operations may also be restricted when opposing forces have local population support as in the case of insurgent hubs (the resurfacing of the M23 rebels may be a case in point). These limitations should be thoroughly considered while developing military options. The options may include utilising regional actors so as to achieve maximum effect through offensive operations.

In considering the efficiency of UN offensive operations in the event of encountering guerrilla/insurgent forces, it may be necessary to combine manoeuvre warfare with counterinsurgency strategies.[63]

---

[63] Baker, D and Jordaan, E (Eds). 2010. *Contemporary Counterinsurgency: Roots, Practices, Prospects.* (Cape Town: University of Cape Town Press); UN Global Counterinsurgency Strategy,https://www.un.org/counterterrorism/ctitf/en/u n-global-counter-terrorism-strategy; K. Friis,

Counterinsurgency can be defined as the "blend of comprehensive civilian and military efforts designed to simultaneously contain insurgency and address its root causes" (US Government, 2009,p. 2). This of course is subject to the mission mandate and is only suggested if the UN decides in pursuing an aggressive military strategy. Should the UN not be willing to decode and decipher the complexity of military doctrine and theory, offensive operations may not be the correct policy tool for executing UN mandates.

Conclusion

The SC's mandate of unilateral offensive operations is in many ways a throwback to the thinking in the conception of the UN Charter which was aimed at countering aggression in the maintenance of international peace (White, 2013, p. 572). Despite the mandate, the UN has until present not effectively defined offensive operations within peacekeeping doctrine. As a result, it is difficult to understand the character and limits of such operations. The decision of the UN to make use of offensive operations necessitates the DPKO/DFS to develop military strategic and operational frameworks to define and efficiently execute offensive operations.

This chapter contributes to the study of UN offensive operations and has proposed a UN military strategic and operational framework, theoretical constructs regarding offensive operations (manoeuvre theory) and suggestions as to amendments to doctrine regarding offensive operations across the level of peacekeeping.

'Peacekeeping and Counter-insurgency – Two of a Kind?', *International Peacekeeping*, 17, 1, 2010.

The chapter suggests that the UN make use of manoeuvre warfare theory as a broad approach to the conduct of offensive operations on the strategic and operational levels of peacekeeping. Furthermore, the chapter suggests that the UN's theoretical approach to war and offensive operations be highlighted in the respective doctrinal publications and manuals. Manoeuvre warfare theory recognises the importance of technology as well as intelligence, counterintelligence and technology.[64] Despite the significance of technology, the most important factor remains leadership and the human element (Vego, 2007,p. XII-28).

The chapter finally suggests that the military underpinnings of combat operations should be clearly stated in the DPKO Capstone Doctrine and should filter down through to the manuals for Infantry, Engineers, Special Forces, Air Support and other military elements. The understanding of offensive operations through a common doctrinal lens will promote interoperability. There is a need for 'joint' doctrine which should clearly outline command relationships, subordinations and organisation.[65]

---

[64] See UN DPKO/DFS, 'Policy: Peacekeeping Intelligence', 2017; O. Abilova and A. Novosseloff, "Demystifying Intelligence in UN Peace Operations: Toward an Organizational Doctrine", *International Peace Institute*, 2016; Expert Panel on Technology and Innovation in UN Peacekeeping, 'Final Report: Performance Peacekeeping', United Nations, 2014; A. Walter Dorn, 'Smart Peacekeeping: Toward Tech-Enabled UN Operations', International Peace Institute, 2016.

[65] This can be similar to a military organisation. See M.N. Vego, *Joint Operational Warfare: Theory and Practice* (Newport: Naval War College, 2007), pp. XII-28.

The path of offensive combat operations is a complex one. The UN should carefully consider this intricacy for two reasons. Firstly, due to the inherent difficulty of fighting under the banner of DPKO, and secondly, because of the challenging precedent that it sets on the political level, whether formally or tacitly.

Chapter 4: United Nations Peacekeeping Offensive Operations: Concepts and Command Centres

The decision to strategically mandate offensive operations in the post-cold war peacekeeping era is for the most part unchartered territory. It will thus require forward thinking and some level of trial and error. Chapter four builds on from the previous chapter, 'United Nations Peacekeeping Offensive Operations: Theory and Doctrine'. Where theory provides a construct for the conduct of operations, doctrine should guide the execution of operations without being overly prescriptive (US, 2014, p. 70). Doctrine provides the 'how to' in the conduct of operations where concepts look to the future of peacekeeping offensive operations.

The study of United Nations peacekeeping offensive operations is at a critical moment, and is highlighted by a higher operational intensity as indicated in the recent battle in Beni. In this city in the north eastern Democratic Republic of the Congo, 15 peacekeepers were killed and approximately 40 were injured. The UN Secretary General Antonio Guterres condemned the attack. He stated unequivocally that, "this is the worst attack on UN peacekeepers in the Organisation's recent history" (SG, 2017). The increasing casualties of UN peacekeepers in Mali as well as the Central African Republic are further examples of a higher operational tempo in African theatres. The aim of this chapter is to put forward a proposed future peacekeeping offensive operations cornerstone and operating concept, and command infrastructure amendments on the strategic and operational levels of peacekeeping.

United Nations Future Peacekeeping Offensive Operations Cornerstone and Operating Concept

This chapter suggests the creation of a future peacekeeping offensive operations cornerstone and operating concept which should guide the application of peacekeeping offensive operations. Concepts consider the use of future capabilities to achieve missions while providing an intellectual foundation for modernisation (US, 2014, p. 7). The cornerstone concept should indicate the UN's overarching philosophy regarding the use of force in peacekeeping. The UN future operating concept should be subordinate to the cornerstone concept, and it should guide the way that UN military forces operate in peacekeeping.

The suggested concepts draw from the practical experience and historical context of the Force Intervention Brigade (FIB) as the first modern offensively mandated UN peacekeeping offensive force. Following the initial success of the FIB in its attainment of strategic and tactical objectives, its performance has been lacklustre. The proposed peacekeeping cornerstone concept could thus provide clarity on the FIB's role and function on the strategic, operational and tactical levels of peacekeeping.

The UN cornerstone and operating concepts should respond to the constantly changing international trends and threats in security and conflict. International security trends have shown a considerable increase of asymmetrical and extremist threats, guerrilla attacks as well as terrorism (Ladsous, 2015; UK, 2012). Examples of this trend include the conflict in Mali and the recent attack in the city of Beni in the DRC. The strategic threat perspective which informs the functioning of the various UN apparatus should guide the UN future strategies for peacekeeping.[66]

The UN foundational and guiding documents on peacekeeping operations provide the basis for the understanding of future concepts. Concepts look forward while doctrine guides the current thinking and practice in operations. The evolution of post-Cold War peacekeeping is demonstrated through the substantial guidance which includes but is not limited to: the 'Brahimi Report' (2000), Capstone Doctrine (2008), 'New Partnership Agenda: Charting a New Horizon for Peacekeeping' (2009), 'Global Field Support Strategy' (2010), 'The Contribution of United Nations Peacekeeping to Early Peacebuilding: A DPKO/DFS Strategy for Peacekeeping' (2011), 'The Planning Toolkit' (2012), 'Strategic Planning in the United Nations System' (2012); 'Under-Secretary-General for Peacekeeping Operations Hervé Ladsous Statement to the Fourth Committee' (2015), and 'Use of Force by Military Components in United Nations Peacekeeping Operations' (2017). Where these documents provide the foundations for strategic understanding, the cornerstone and operating concepts should inform forecasted trends in conflict and the UN's proposed response.

The UN cornerstone concept should be inextricably intertwined with force generation planning and philosophies.[67] Force generation strategies are principally concerned with quantities and not necessarily military capabilities (Smith, 2013) by which it addresses

---

[66] See UN, "The Contribution of United Nations Peacekeeping to Early Peacebuilding: A DPKO/DFS Strategy for Peacekeeping", 2011.

[67] See A. Smith and A. Boutellis, 'Rethinking Force Generation: Filling the Capability Gaps in UN Peacekeeping, *International Peace Institute*, 2013.

the 'means' of future peacekeeping. This chapter builds on the thinking surrounding force generation and the acquisition of capabilities for future peace missions.

Future conflict trends are likely to be marked by uncertainty and further complexity in operations. The cornerstone concept should envision the future aims and threats to future operations as well as the means and ways to overcome challenges and achieve mission objectives. In so doing, the concept should shape the way that the UN leadership think about future peacekeeping operations. The UN cornerstone concept will thus guide future peacekeeping forces' knowledge and understanding of future threats and challenges while preparing them for peacekeeping operations.[68]

The proposed title for the future UN peacekeeping offensive operations cornerstone concept is proposed as: Adaptable offensive operations: neutralising armed groups in complex international contexts.[69] The cornerstone concept should thus indicate higher level ends and ways, while highlighting strategic intent. This proposed concept ties in with the strategic intent of the United Nations Security Council (UNSC) as stated in Resolution 2348, which mandated the neutralisation of Armed Groups in the DRC through

---

[68] A comparison can be made with a military capstone concept which aims to prepare military forces to face future threats: Association of the US Army, 'Defence Report: The U.S. Army Capstone Concept: Defining the Army of 2020', *Institute of Land Warfare*, 2013, p. 1.

[69] The suggested UN future peacekeeping offensive operations cornerstone concept requires further research and analysis so as to be developed into a complete document.

offensive operations, to be "robust, highly mobile and versatile" (UN, 2017:11). The thoughts of Hervé Ladsous, the Under Secretary General (USG) of peacekeeping, echoes this sentiment. He asserts the necessity of "adapting our capabilities and our field support to allow Missions to act in an agile, mobile, robust and pre-emptive manner" (Ladsous, 2015,).[70] The UN peacekeeping offensive operations cornerstone concept should then be linked to the UN peacekeeping offensive operations operating concept.

The UN peacekeeping offensive operations operating concept should address the forecasted practicalities of future missions while focussing on the operational level of peacekeeping. This operating concept should be based on the changing character of the peace and security landscape.[71] Furthermore, the UN peacekeeping offensive operations operating concept addresses any obstacles to operational efficiency. In so doing, the operating concept should guide the organisation's philosophical approach in dealing with current and future operations.

USG Ladsous, in a statement to the Fourth Committee, referred to the 'challenges of operating effectively in new environments'. He cited the complexity and robust nature of three particular operations. These are MONUSCO in the DRC, the United Nations Multidimensional Integrated Stabilisation Mission in the Central

---

[70] See A. Garcia, 'United Nations Peacekeeping Offensive Operations: Theory and Doctrine', *Small Wars Journal*, September 2017.

[71] A comparison is made with the military operating concept which is based on the character of future war: UK Army, *Joint Concept Note 2/12l Future Land Operating Concept* (Swindon: Ministry of Defence, 2012), pp. 1-7.

African Republic (MINUSCA) and the United Nations Multidimensional Integrated Stabilisation Mission in Mali (MINUSMA). Ladsous further highlighted the limitations of rugged terrain. Such geographical challenges are augmented by determined attacks of Armed Groups utilising small arms and increasingly sophisticated improvised explosive devices (IEDs) (Ladsous, 2015). The increased operational intensity of UN peacekeeping in Africa indicates the need for a clear concept for future operations.

The proposed UN offensive peacekeeping operating concept considers one of the primary objectives of peacekeeping which is fundamentally linked to Protection of Civilians (POC). The proposed UN peacekeeping offensive operations operating concept links offensive operations - the neutralising of Armed Groups as stipulated in UN SC Resolution 2348, with POC (UN, 2017, p. 11). Without military control of an area, it would be difficult for civilian peacekeepers to effectively operate and achieve POC objectives. The recent attack by UN FIB forces outside Beni in the DRC where 15 Tanzanian soldiers were killed and approximately 40 were injured, is a case in point. In a situation where an active, aggressive and reasonably well organised armed group caries out harassing operations, it becomes increasingly difficult for civilian peacekeepers to effectively carry out their function in support of a POC mandate.

The UN peacekeeping offensive operations operating concept should focus on the tactical realities and obstacles within the operational theatre. Thus the proposed UN operating concept should address complex tactical issues. These include crucial capabilities such as air support and engineer units, which as force multipliers assist in overcoming complex physical and human terrain.[72]

A suggested title for the proposed future UN peacekeeping offensive operations operating concept is, Enabling protection of civilians through mobile operations in complex peacekeeping environments.[73] A case that supports this concept was the neutralisation of the M23 which in turn enabled MONUSCO to resume their POC mandate. It further promoted regional accountability in response to a crisis. The UN future peacekeeping offensive operations operating concept should guide the future operations of the FIB and UN elements in support of combat operations (for example in Mali). It should also act as a model for other peace missions such as those in South Sudan, Darfur and the CAR.

The strategic level command should ensure that the UN offensive force has the resources and mandate to achieve the required combat objectives. Based on the strategic objectives, the operational level must conceptualise and plan the required campaigns through operational art. In this regard, the UN has made great strides in its work towards standby forces, strategic force generation and rapidly deployable brigades. Where national Departments of Defence

---

[72] See UN, "Draft Lessons Learned: Study on FIB Operations", 2014; H. Ladsous, "Statement of Under-Secretary-General for Peacekeeping Operations to the Fourth Committee", 2015.

[73] The proposed UN future peacekeeping operating concept requires further research and analysis so as to be developed into a complete document.

develop their strategic vision with national interests in mind,[74] regional military bodies such as the NATO develop their strategic concept considering regional security objectives and concerns.[75] Similarly and more broadly, the UN should develop its future peacekeeping cornerstone and operating concept to address complex missions worldwide.

Proposed Amended UN DPKO/DFS Command Infrastructure for Peacekeeping Offensive Operations

The choice to make use of offensive operations requires the UN to have specific methods to command, control and manage the execution of such operations on the various levels of peacekeeping. One can draw a comparison between war and peacekeeping offensive

---

[74] See US Army, *TRADOC Pamphlet 525-3-1 The US Army Operating Concept, Win in a Complex World 2020 - 2040* (Fort Eustis: TRADOC Publications, 2014); SA Army Vision 2020 Team, *SA Army Strategic Profile* (Pretoria: SA Army HQ, 2006); Australian Army, *Army's Future Land Operating Concept: Adaptive Campaigning* (Canberra: Australian Army HQ, 2009; US Army, *US Army Capstone Concept: Draft Version 2.7* (Fort Eustis: TRADOC Publications, 2009).

[75] See NATO, *NATO Strategic Concept*, 2010. The strategic concept for NATO is currently under revision. This is the result of a change in international threats, terrorism, migration and other factors. For an in-depth analysis on UN-NATO inter-organisation dynamics see M.F. Harsch, *The Power of Dependence, NATO-UN Cooperation in Crisis Management* (Oxford: Oxford University Press, 2015).

operations in that they "are not won or lost on the tactical level but at the strategic and operational levels" (Vego, 2015, p. 60). The Tactics, Techniques and Procedures (TTPs) of Troop Contributing Countries (TCCs) – which feature at the tactical level – are of less importance than the strategic and operational considerations. Furthermore, the choice of a combat-oriented commander who can execute offensive operations is critical to the success of the mission.[76]

Strategic Command Centre

Peacekeeping missions are headed by the SG and the respective force commanders and Special Representatives of the Secretary General (SRSG). The strategic level is thus comprised of the SG, the USGs and relevant departments.[77] Where the SC determines the mandate objectives, the strategic leadership guides mandate implementation.

This chapter thus proposes that a small strategic command centre or cell be created, or amended from existing resources, for specific command, control and guidance of mandated offensive operations at HQ level. The proposed strategic command centre will assist the higher leadership by providing legal and doctrinal guidance and staff analyses. Furthermore, the centre will assist in advising the SG and the SC on the challenges, strategic options and the operationalisation of mandate objectives. There is a definite link between a particular mission's success and the balance of resources, context, leadership and operational realities.

---

[76]   See M. Vego, "On Operational Leadership" *Joint Forces Quarterly*, 77, 2, 2015.

[77]   These may include the DPKO, DFS, OMA, and Integrated Operations Teams.

A prime example is the history of MONUSCO and its predecessor, the United Nations Organisation Mission in the Democratic Republic of the Congo (MONUC). Both have experienced success and failure in utilising offensive operations. The experience of previous MONUSCO force headquarters command and staff has been inclined towards multidimensional peacekeeping with limited offensive operations. It could be argued that the success and commitment to combat operations is subjective to the risk appetite of the respective commanders, TCCs and Security General.[78] Cammaert's proactive leadership against rebel groups in the DRC in 2005 is an example of the effective results which can be achieved with a combination of a suitable force commander and capable blue helmets (Baker & Jordaan, 2010, p. 152). By ensuring military security, the mission is able to continue with the implementation of POC and other mandate objectives.

The proposed strategic command centre could assist in advising the SG and SC on the probabilities of success and failure of offensive operations in a given context, and provide doctrinal guidance on it (this is subject to the creation of doctrine for UN offensive operations across the levels of peacekeeping).[79] This point becomes even more crucial as peacekeeping missions are deployed and made

---

[78] See F. Blyth, and P. Cammaert, "Using Force to Protect Civilians in United Nations Peacekeeping Operations", Chapter in H. Willmot, R. Mamiya, S. Sheeran, and M. Weller, *Protection of Civilians*. Oxford: Oxford University Press, 2016).

[79] See A. Garcia, 'United Nations Peacekeeping Offensive Operations: Theory and Doctrine', *Small Wars Journal*, September 2017.

to take on complex security challenges by being introduced to and forced to operate in combat and combat support roles against asymmetric and other guerrilla threats.

On the topic of operating in complex environments, the US Army states that, "strategic leaders must have some grasp of the ongoing debate about cultural diversity and the understanding of war in fundamentally differing cultural contexts" (US Army, 2001, p. 22). As such, the strategic leadership must have a broad vision and clear understanding of the mission context (Vego, 2015, p. 60). Strategic guidance thus informs the operational level of war and provides options in terms of the balance of ends, ways and means, which historically has always been considered a difficult task (Jablonsky, 1987,p. 65). The UN has a daunting task in providing strategic guidance to offensive mandated operations which may include cooperation with regional partners. The UN's institutional culture and values are different to that of other regional actors such as NATO, which has, on previous occasions led to a challenging partnership in dealing with violent conflict (Harsch, 2015). The compatibility of UN, regional and TCC security infrastructure is a fundamentally important consideration, and becomes a central point in the operationalisation of strategic objectives.

The proposed strategic command centre will thus further inform and guide the operational level of peacekeeping. Where the Rules of Engagement, Status of Force Agreement and CONOPS (UN DPKO/DFS, 2008,p. 14) are often decided at the start of a mission, the operational level should continuously guide, balance and adjust mission objectives between the changing continuum of tactical execution and the fluctuating strategic landscape.

The SC Resolution 2348 (2017) indicated specific strategic military objectives to be attained through offensive operations in the

DRC. In order to achieve these strategic objectives, the aims, as indicated by the SC, must be operationalised. The primary responsibility to operationalise these objective lies within the UN Secretariat, DPKO/DFS, Mission leadership and the Force headquarters. There is also a command imperative from the TCC national commands who are stakeholders in the mission. The CONOPS is discussed and formed with TCCs during the strategic force generation process. It is important to ensure continuity from the creation of the CONOPS to the implementation phase in theatre. In this regard, senior personnel of TCCs who were involved in the mission planning and CONOPS should have appointments at the proposed strategic command centre.

Operational Command Centres

This chapter postulates that the Force headquarters of missions mandated specifically for offensive operations, be further developed to include a broad command centre. Operational staff in such a centre should have the specific function of developing military options for tactical execution. The aforementioned operational command centre could be linked to the G3[80] but should be made up exclusively of TCCs mandated for offensive operations. This will contribute to the overall efficiency of the mission. The envisioned operational level command centre and staff section will also increase efficiency in the provision of logistics and the management of resources. Furthermore, this staff section should not exist in isolation

---

[80]   The G3 is the military staff compartment dealing with operations.

but should form part of the Force command staff and possibly the senior management team.

This chapter does not presume to dictate how the proposed amendment to the operational and strategic command be set up, but rather accentuates their importance. Where offensive operations are mandated, the strategic command centre could be created at the headquarters (New York City or regional country). The operational command centre and staff compartment for offensive operations could then be created at the respective mission headquarters.

The operational level in peacekeeping must inform the tactical level in terms of attaining strategic mandate objectives. The proposed operational level of command in peacekeeping is based on the operational level in war which is designed to "determine the sequence of actions most likely to produce the military conditions that will achieve the strategic goals" (Jablonsky, 1987, p. 65). Operational commanders in peacekeeping should think operationally and not tactically. They should thus be able to build a strategic and operational picture of the theatre of operations which addresses military and non-military aspects that influence the mission (Vego, 2015, p. 62).

This chapter thus proposes that the UN create a command centre and operational staff compartment for offensive operations which will be necessary to determine the tasks required in order to achieve the SC's mandate objectives. UN offensive operations within multidimensional peacekeeping missions are generally low intensity when compared to conventional wars of attrition. In cases of lower intensity operations, the operational level is usually smaller than in high intensity conflict (Vego, 2007, pp. XII-28). The operational thinking on this level of peacekeeping informs the operational vision which determines the centres of gravity of the opposing force (Vego

2015, p. 62). UN missions with offensive mandates, such as the FIB, should thus have a small operational command centre and staff compartment. The section should steer tactical execution by neutralising the Armed Groups' centres of gravity/critical vulnerability. These steps should be put into effect in order to achieve strategic objectives as part of the broader mission.[81]

Conclusion

This chapter proposes the creation of a future peacekeeping offensive operations cornerstone and operating concepts which should guide the application of force in peacekeeping operations. The cornerstone concept should guide the UN's overarching philosophy regarding the use of force in peacekeeping. The operating concept should guide the way that UN military forces operate in offensive peacekeeping missions.

The proposed title for the future UN peacekeeping offensive operations cornerstone concept is Adaptable offensive operations: neutralising armed groups in complex international contexts. A suggested title for the future UN peacekeeping offensive operations operating concept is Enabling protection of civilians through mobile operations in complex peacekeeping environments.

---

[81]   NATO exclusively deploys Joint operational level headquarters, whether in peace enforcement or conventional operations: M. H. Clemmesen, 'Present and Future Command Structure: A Finish View', Chapter in T. Young, *Command in NATO after the Cold War: Alliance, National and Multinational Considerations*, (Carlisle: Strategic Studies Institute, 1997)p. 196.

The chapter suggests that the UN make a minor amendment to the strategic and operational command centres, so as to include staff exclusively dedicated to mandated offensive operations. These members of staff will assist the strategic and operational commanders in operationalising strategic objectives, facilitating CONOPS, and advising the SG and SC on critical failings, strategic options, challenges, and combat mandates.

Chapter 5: Entanglement of Military Theory in Peacekeeping, Ancient Roots and Modern Fruits

This work aims to extend current military theoretical concepts into the field of offensive peacekeeping operations. When considering offensive peacekeeping operations, the following questions need to be asked: Should the Clausewitzian phrase that war is the continuation of politics be adopted? Does the FIB thus represent the continuation of regional politics by other means? Lastly, have the tactical actions of the FIB resulted in the political objectives of the AU and the UN? This is not always a linear question in international relations as the objectives and interests of armed groups, civilian populations and international supporters are not always clear.

In order to ensure that there is a connection between the political objectives and the tactical execution, the practitioners on the ground and the strategic level should understand the end game. This book discusses how strategy and tactics work in offensive peacekeeping operations and identifies gaps in operational doctrine where further guidance is required.

The topic of UN offensive peacekeeping operations is of great importance to the South African National Defence Force. The present determines how we will deploy in the future. This often requires a new analysis of past operations. There is a considerable space for analysis and discovery depending on the object of the military theoretical enquiry.

Manoeuvre theory and attrition theory are two broad military theories that have been used throughout millennia of warfare. The two theories are not mutually exclusive and are often both found or applied in different contexts. They are used to explain and understand war and this can be transferred to offensive peacekeeping operations. In previous chapters, this book has proposed that the UN should adopt a formal military theory for offensive peacekeeping operations. It also suggests the use of manoeuvre theory in a similar vein to how NATO has applied the theory.

Manoeuvre theory as a method of warfare comprises the basic idea of defeating your enemy through the least amount of effort and with attaining the least loss possible. Manoeuvre is regarded by many as the most important means of achieving victory in conflict (Solberg, 2000, p. 21). Attrition and manoeuvre theory are the basic yet most prominent theories applied to conventional warfare. Both are directed at defeating the opposing force.

The theories on unconventional warfare such as guerrilla warfare have similar concepts and underlying foundations to manoeuvre theory. The history of guerrilla and irregular warfare dates back to biblical times. As an example, the book of Joshua refers to the Israeli conquest of Canaan (Ellis, 1995, p. 17).

Eastern thought on the conduct of war and the pursuit of victory via the easiest means possible is congruent to that of manoeuvre warfare. The Eastern approach to strategy and military theory emphasises balance and harmony as important characteristics to be considered in the offensive and defensive. Sun Tzu compares the quest for success to the flow of water, which is shapeless. Water follows the lay of the land and courses around obstacles as opposed to being blocked by them (Tzu, 1994, p. 5). Many of the concepts expounded on by Tzu are similar to that of manoeuvre warfare theory (Solberg, 2000, p. 5). Tzu states that, "water shapes its path according to the nature of the ground and a soldier in terms of the enemy." (Tzu, 1994, p. 13). The mind of the commander should thus be shapeless like water. The more fluid the commander's mind is the greater comprehension s/he will have of the large scale from the small scale (strategic to tactical). (Musashi, 2006, p. 10).

The principles of manoeuvre warfare theory underpin the readiness of a military force and the attainment of victory with the least amount of human and material loss. War is, of course, the result of politics. The attainment of a rapid and favourable peace following the war is the ultimate object. In a long war, there is more material loss as well as life loss on both sides, which is rarely the object of political planning.

I believe that military strategic studies is at its core a practical subject. The use of history and theory in the military environment equips students of conflict with a conceptual understanding of past campaigns, peacekeeping missions, operations and wars. This provides a great source of knowledge to the practising soldier, as most military practitioners will most likely not have the opportunity to experience many theatres of operations in their lifetime. Liddell Hart has proposed direct and indirect experience as methods from which soldiers may gather knowledge and understanding of the profession of arms (Liddell Hart, 1941, p. 2).

Through the study of military history, certain theories and principles have been extracted in terms of war and its methods. Principles of war in South Africa are described as, "a fundamental truth governing the prosecution of war… and must be understood in their entirety, not as dogma to be rigidly applied." (SANDF, 2004, p. 33). Every country has its own principles of war and the principles of war across nations generally have similar aspects. Perhaps this indicates a certain universality and wisdom, which is shared by many on paper but applied by few in practice.

The peace and security analysis in this work has been influenced by current political scholarly trends in conflict. This book provides a combination of theory and conceptual modelling and falls within the specialised field of military theory which was popularised in the Cold War era. The understanding of the different theories of war and its applications is of utmost importance to soldiers, politicians and armchair strategists alike.

The current preponderance of war in the world and the tactics used in peacekeeping missions has led me to question the methods, operational art and strategy used in current peacekeeping operations. In questioning the methods, it is important to consider past South African Peacekeeping Operations (PKO) to determine the way forward. The South African military takes a maneouverist approach to conventional warfare and its training is largely directed at mobile operations, which are designed for a short duration. The question is: what is the approach when it comes to peacekeeping? Where military theorists and practitioners dedicate a large amount of time to the study of war, an unequal amount of time is dedicated to the analysis of PKO. With the advent of UN mandated offensive operations, and SA's role as a key TCC, this should be a key consideration.

Military theory has various components. These include the human/psychological, political and scientific/technological aspects. Rather than being hard and fast components of war, these are fluid and flexible facets. Military history and the military experience of a nation, country or state also serves to derive principles of war. Most countries have some form of 'principles of war'. Manoeuvre is a principle of war in the South African military.

Manoeuvre as a principle of war is described as, "a fundamental truth regarding the prosecution of war... the object is to dispose a force in such a manner as to place the enemy at a relative disadvantage and achieve results that would otherwise be costly in men and material" (SANDF, 2004, p. 40). Besides following the principle of manoeuvre, the SANDF also ascribes to the manoeverist approach in terms of war theory. This work pays special attention to observing the tradition of manoeuvre. Accordingly, it puts forth that where required, the UN offensive peacekeeping forces use manoeuvre warfare as a means to achieve its objectives.

The idea of using manoeuvre and instances where it has been used to influence battles and operations can be found throughout history. Manoeuvre does not refer only to physical movement. It has the effect of destroying opponents' will to fight by the execution of movements and action. These result in a sensory overload, which promotes confusion and moral breakdown. Hence, manoeuvre applies to the physical and human/social/psychological realms.

Great generals and commanders have demonstrated awareness of this utilisation of manoeuvre. Across history, there are examples of military brilliance which have incorporated aspects of manoeuvre theory. The Battle of Pharsalus, for example, was a contest between the military genius of Julius Caesar and Gnaeus Pompeius (Pompey). Caesar won the battle decisively through the use of envelopment and guile, resulting in the routing of Pompey's force. Caesar's forces had major logistical and supply difficulties and were desperate.

Manoeuvre warfare theory is not merely a case of envelopment of the enemy (as executed by Caesar). It involves outthinking the opponent and capturing and maintaining the initiative so that the enemy is always reactive. Many great commanders throughout history have made use of ingenious ways to defeat their opponents. Included are Hannibal, Saladin, Napoleon and Ghenghis Khan, to name but a few. Envelopment, flanking attacks, direct attacks and surprise attacks are all part of the theory of manoeuvre. Manoeuvre theory is fundamentally linked to attrition theory which promotes the use of direct attack, firepower and the massing of forces in the Jominian, Clausewitzian and Napoleonic mould.

Abel Esterhuyse discusses the relationship between attrition and manoeuvre theory with regards to the levels of war (Esterhuyse, 2001, p. 86). He states that the levels of warfare influence the extent to which the different theories become intertwined. The SANDF 'Staff Officers Operational Manual' also emphasises the interconnection between manoeuvre and attrition theory (SA, 1996,p 7/3-2). The different theories of war have been debated in military academies and colleges across the world. The relevant importance of military theories and their practicality in the execution of war is still hotly debated. At the present time, military theorists should determine how war theories and their application applies to offensive peacekeeping operations. Generals and Special Representatives to the Secretary General, along with their staff, must determine how best to apply military theory in this time of social media connectivity and its effect on public opinion.

The principle, methods and tactics employed in the history of combat have been and still are based on the practicalities of warfare. Theories on war are largely the conceptual frameworks which commanders rely on in their approach to plan and execute war. Despite the realities on the ground and the frictions which surround offensive operations, the commander should remain of sound mind at all times whereby the tactical realm is understood within the operational and strategic context.

There are three main levels of war, namely the strategic, operational and tactical levels. The strategic level is where political objectives are determined. This may be regional, national, or international. The operational level is specific to a front, mission or campaign and may be a peacekeeping mission. The tactical level includes battles, patrols and skirmishes (Leonhard, 1994, p. 6).

Manoeuvre warfare as a theory is flexible and can be applied on different scales. Manoeuvre warfare extends itself over the three levels of war (Solberg, 2000, p. 5). Violence should be used as a calculated action so as to attain the acquired result.

At the present time, we need to develop sustainable ideas and theories on peacekeeping. How much overlap exists between peacekeeping theory and the theories of war? Where there is a definite psychological facet, is it completely transferable?

Colonel Ardant Du Picq was a French military theorist and operational officer who promulgated his theories on the study of morale and unit cohesion in combat (Du Picq, 2005). He was indirectly influenced by the Napoleonic era and the theories put forth by his predecessors Jomini and Clausewitz. Du Picq stated that weapons are central in influencing the morale of the enemy.'(Leonhard, 1994, p. 44). Jomini was of the opinion that where weaponry may increase the possibility to achieve victory in war, it is not directly proportional to win battles (Parker, 1995, p. 2). Where the FDLR and ADF suffer limited casualties, there is no indication that their morale has collapsed.

Clausewitz alludes to the difficulties in war which he terms as 'friction'. He states that it is not possible to define this friction on paper, but only through the practice of warfare, and that it is intrinsically related to chance in warfare (Von Clausewitz, 2006, p. 43). Friction may include but is not limited to physical exertion, danger, intelligence and uncertainty (Solberg, 2000, p. 22). In the mind of the soldier, the psychological effect or real and perceived danger is almost identical (Gal and Mangelsdorff, 1991, p. 511). The strategic objectives of campaigns are influenced by friction across the levels of war.

Clausewitz's colossal tome 'On war' is perhaps the most complete work on the theoretical underpinnings of warfare. Clausewitz and Liddell Hart have defined strategy in a similar manner, referring to the military means which are used to fulfill political ends (Holmes, 2001, p. 879). Strategic aims become operational objectives and then tactical objectives. Should battle be accepted or chosen, military operations are shifted into the realm of tactics. On the tactical level, manoeuvre and attrition theories are interwoven where manoeuvre is translated into mobility and attrition into firepower (Esterhuyse, 2001, p. 91). Manoeuvre is most effective on the operational level as firepower is tactically more decisive (Simkin, 1986, p. 23). The question that must be answered by SRSGs and Force Commanders, however, is how tactical actions can secure strategic objectives.

Clausewitz's contribution to the understanding of war includes his analysis on the nature of war and how its nature endures even as its character changes (Gray, 2007, p. 15). Gray states that if the nature of war changes, it would become something else. The character of war is thus susceptible to change with respect to the situation (Gray, 2005, p. 16). In the modern context, generals, senior staff, and high ranking civilian UN officials must determine how this applies with the increased significance on non-state actors.

Military commanders and political and civilian leaders must identify the objectives of a mission. In the case of the UN offensive peacekeeping operations, various TCCs and resources should be dedicated to achieving the objectives of the mission. The political and economic aspects of peacekeeping mandates should also be balanced. The process for an international polyglot force to achieve UN objectives is complex. The CONOPS and strategic guidance as well as force regeneration should be tightly knit with the strategic interests and objectives of the Security Council and the Nation States involved. The deployment and application of forces in an offensively mandated peacekeeping mission must be able to achieve strategic and political objectives through aggressive actions.

The strategic level of war and offensive peacekeeping operations is the highest level for the planning of combat and as such determines the objectives of the operational level. The operational level has components of military art and science. It is on this level that offensive peacekeeping operations should take place. The operational level must direct its efforts at achieving the strategic objectives. The operational level objectives must be executed on the tactical and lowest planning level of war. The tactical level involves the battles and engagement that wins campaigns. Battles that are fought must be directly related to the achievement of the objectives of the operational level and in turn the achievement of the strategic objectives. If this is not the case, the battles are a waste of resources, and possibly lives and time (Leonhard, 1994, pp. 7-10). Regarding the situation in the DRC, the question is: how does the FIB defeat the ADF, LRA and FDLR?

Each level of war should therefore be assigned a relative and proportional centre of gravity according to the precepts of military science. Accordingly, military strategy is a means to attain political ends and not military ends as an end onto itself. In this regard, the undisclosed caveats of TCCs may impact the SC's mandates. The collective understanding of the political ends through military means influences the tactical dimension as the understanding of the operational level allows for tactical success and operational victory.

When operations are conducted, there are certain decisive points. In the case of offensive peacekeeping operation where there is not always a conventional opponent to face, these decisive points are not always comprised of well-defended positions with hard point targets, but may take a different form. Hearts and minds, information operations, protection of civilians and other methods may be required in a setting where irregular warfare is used. This type of operations may have some similarity to counter-insurgency and asymmetric warfare. Militaries need to dedicate sufficient time to studying UN offensive operations. This is because it is a field that is different to other types of peacekeeping operations.

Militaries are generally trained in conventional and unconventional war fighting. Peacekeeping, however, is often treated with a mild neglect. This is in part be related to the idea that peacekeeping is 'softer' than more traditional operations, or because less political capital is generally invested in them. As a result, militaries spend the majority of their time training for war and counter-insurgency operations. It would be a good idea for governments and militaries to develop training capabilities for UN offensive peacekeeping operations. Such an initiative would require coordination with the DPK so as to allow for the coordination of models, concepts, doctrine and expectations. The key to UN offensive operations is to determine the centre of gravity of the armed groups which must be neutralised.

In conventional war, the operational level centre of gravity is often a headquarters (HQ), which governs, commands and directs the forces (Leonhard, 1994, pp. 20-23). In operations other than war, it is more difficult to identify the centre of gravity. This is because the centre of gravity could be an ideology or belief, and hence is often intangible. Clausewitz believed the centre of gravity to be related to the centre of mass, which was at the time widely regarded as the strongest point in the enemy (Solberg, 2000, p. 26). This was the method required to achieve victory between massed armies and to effect political intent.

The concept of a focussed attack of massed armies is not always the approach pursued in warfare, and even less so in offensively mandated peacekeeping operations. The centre of gravity in conventional warfare could take various forms, such as the political or military headquarters or capital city of a country. This would be the strategic centre of gravity. An operational centre of gravity, however, could be a railway centre or key terrain, which allows for the attainment of the strategic objective. In operations other than war and asymmetric warfare, key terrain may be something intangible such as gaining the trust of local communities.

The tactical centre of gravity could be a 'smaller' objective, such as defeating a given force grouping so as to get access to the operational objective and centre of gravity. Theoretically, a series of tactical objectives leads to an operational objective. Ideally the movement of military forces could negate the extensive use of direct contact. It battles with the opposing force so as to achieve operational objectives with less material and life loss. Despite the theoretical model, the sometimes painful reality is that certain strategic objectives do not have a tactical solution (Lawrence, 1935, p. 197). This is never more evident than in guerrilla warfare, insurgency, terrorism and asymmetric warfare. Contemporary peacekeeping contexts may be influenced by a range of factors and destabilisers including non-state actors, violent extremists, rebels, criminal bands, illegal trade and disaffected national forces.

In considering the strategy and approach to achieving successful offensive peacekeeping operations, one has to consider direct and indirect options. Liddell Hart refers to the indirect strategy as a philosophical truth that can be applied in life and in war. He goes on to describe the importance of evading the direct attack on enemy defensive positions so as to avoid an alternative enveloping or surprise attack (Liddell Hart, 1941).

Liddell Hart deliberates on the chief incalculable element of war, human will and how the dual elements of mobility and surprise are key to physical and combat cohesion and influencing victory in battle (Liddell Hart, 1967). Indirect strategy can also be applied in offensive peacekeeping operations. These are, however, limited by the resources available and political caveats of diverse TCCs.

An indirect strategy in offensive peacekeeping operation may also include humanitarian work and efforts to win the hearts and minds of the local population. The principles of an indirect strategy should also be proportional to that of the principles of war of the TCCs carrying out the operations.

The South African principles of war include manoeuvre and surprise, which are comprised of rapidity, originality, secrecy and deception (SANDF, 2004, p. 35). Surprise often results in panic and a feeling of searching for immediate escape (Glad, 1990, p. 229). These principles have been used successfully in various campaigns in South Africa's rich military history. Included among these are the First World War German South West African and German East African campaigns, the Second World War East and North African campaigns as well as the South African War and the 1914 Afrikaner Rebellion. Mobile warfare was also applied during the various phases of the South African Border War.

Surprise and manoeuvre should thus aim to dislocate enemy forces and psychologically impair their commanders (Simkin, 1986, p. 30). When this happens, the retreating force will withdraw until a place where a strong defensive position can be held or until where it is reinforced with reserves (Von Clausewitz, 2006, p. 133).

In the instance of irregular warfare, rebels may attack a position or commit an act of violence against the population and then retreat to a safe space when facing a counter attack by UN forces. In this case, it is important for the UN to have a prompt response and access to complex terrain. The use of a rapid reaction force with helicopters could assist in this regard. The effects of retreating and being surrounded could lead to a blow to the morale of rebel forces.

In choosing a force commander for a UN mission, the stakeholders should take into account the importance of having a well-respected, feared and accomplished commander. The thought of facing great and competent commanders such as Napoleon or Rommel in their prime, inspired fear in many of their opponents. Where spoilers and armed groups do not respect the UN peacekeeping forces and their commander, disaster is sure to follow. A case in point is the invasion of Goma by the M23 in 2012.

There is also a need for the great generals to reassert their position in the modern context. Generals should have clear and defined objectives, and are only as good as the forces under their command. The conduct of operations should also be framed by a theory of war and a doctrine. In the case UN offensive peacekeeping operations, this is complicated because of the various nationalities involved in the conflict. The work at hand puts forward the idea of using manoeuvre warfare and the timeless maxims of military theory in the application of UN offensive peacekeeping forces.

Two essential maxims have proven to be of great importance. They are the line of least resistance and the line of least expectation. The former deals with the physical and psychological aspects of warfare, and the latter is linked to surprise. The line of least resistance often refers to geographical and tactical considerations. Morale is essential to the attainment of victory in battle (Du Picq,, 2005, p. 70). The psychological dimension of warfare is a balancing act between the morale of own and opposing forces. These maxims serve as a general guide to the conduct of military campaigns and should also apply to UN offensive peacekeeping operations.

Moral surprise refers to where the enemy is unaware of an imminent attack (Simkin, 1986,p. 182). A case in point is during the Second World War when the French considered the Ardennes to be impenetrable. This resulted in surprise and dislocation when the Germans passed through the Ardennes, attacking their forces (SA, 1996,p. 7/5-10). Manoeuvre warfare attempts to do the unexpected, thereby gaining the initiative from the enemy. Jomini states that the massing of forces on decisive points whereby the initiative is gained is essential for victory (Jomini, 2007, p. 54).

In the case of UN offensive peacekeeping operations, the application of surprise can be put into effect through rapid attacks and envelopments using airpower as well as building roads through the dense Ituri Rainforest in the north eastern DRC. The military actions should be followed up by civilian sections – civil affairs, human rights section and political affairs – so as to ensure a holistic effort. Political actions should correspond to and complement military initiatives. The entire mission should be top down in that the military forces aim to achieve the political objectives.

In seeking to achieve political aims, military forces have to seize the initiative. Conflict and military theories often speak of gaining and keeping the initiative. Musashi refers to this as pre-emption, which is achieved by attacking your opponent on your own initiative (Musahi, 2006, p. 48). Peacekeeping contexts often have periods of extensive calm. The tranquility is followed by attacks, abuses and displacement, which are once again followed by periods of calm. This is the nature of low intensity conflict where there are attacks with irregular frequency. Forces should thus be able to pre-empt or respond to such attacks in such a way that defeats an enemy force and deters future acts of aggression. Air mobility for trooping of forces, air assault gunships and rapid response are essential to this type of model. Intelligence and early warning systems as well as a rehearsed and trained military are also vital for effective reaction to such attacks.

Colonel John Boyd's decision cycle or OODA – observation, orientation, decision, action, (Leonhard, 1994, p. 51) can be used to gain the initiative. The upper hand can be achieved by completing this cycle before the enemy and by effect disrupting the OODA cycle of the enemy (Solberg, 2000, p. 21). The OODA loop and attainment and loss of the initiative occur at the various levels of war. A case in point regarding initiative at the strategic level was mentioned by Benito Mussolini. He was talking about the North African campaign during the Second World War and said, "I told Hitler we had lost the initiative from June 1942 onwards, and that a nation which has lost the initiative has lost the war" (Barnett, 2004, p. 251).

In the case of the FIB in the DRC, the Brigade regained the initiative by defeating the M23. On the strategic level, however, various objectives were added to the mandate which were not necessarily achievable with the military means available. As a result, the FIB and MONUSCO lost the initiative. The FIB was formed as the result of countries in sub-Saharan Africa opposing Rwandan backed spoilers M23 in Eastern DRC. The result was that regional political players including South Africa, Tanzania and Malawi agreed to put boots on the ground to back up their political stance. Their forces were accordingly deployed to achieve their political objectives.

Where the neutralising of M23 was regarded as a political requirement for regional political players. The subsequent UNSC mandated objectives of defeating the ADF, FDLR, and LRA, were perhaps not regarded with equal importance. The reasonably quick result in the defeat of the M23 gave the world the impression that the objectives of UN offensive peacekeeping operations are 'easily' achievable. This may in fact be true when facing a rebel threat that takes on a shape similar to a conventional force. In such a case, traditional military theory, doctrine, and tactics can be applied. In the instance of an insurgent force, the operational situation becomes more layered and complex and it is more challenging to execute a counter-insurgency for which the UN has no mandate.

The application of such operations may be subject to UN doctrine and theory and to that of the TCCs. The components of doctrine includes national culture, the influence of formative experiences and the organisational and institutional interests. These are as essential aspects to the formation of military doctrine (Gooch, 1996, p. 6).

The South African military experience has had a definitive effect on the formation of a South African military doctrine. The Afrikaner experience of warfare led to the formation of institutions such as the commando system, which had an influence on the way in which they fought. The formation of commandos was the result of the Afrikaner military experience. The influence of the British military tradition added a more formal element to that of the South African military. The tradition of manoeuvre has been present in South African campaigns from the South African War, the German South West African campaign, and the German East African Campaign (both First World War) to the Second World War campaigns in East and

North Africa as well as the South African Border War. The Struggle and independence in 1994 ushered in a new era for the SA military where non-statutory forces, APLA and MK amalgamated with the SADF to form the SANDF.

The military experience of the ANC and APLA took shape for the most part in insurgency and guerrilla warfare. The conventional aspect of military operations was not studied by all members of the former guerrilla forces. In the post-1994 era, during the amalgamation of the various forces, the focus was mostly on conventional training and force preparation. The result was a combination of a technically efficient conventional soldiers, and politically savvy guerilla soldiers.

With Thabo Mbeki's drive towards safety, security and development in Africa, the SANDF took on a new role in the post-1994 environment. Since then, the South African military has mainly assumed a peacekeeping role, although there was a stabilisation mission in Lesotho in 1998 and a deployment into the Central African Republic in 2012, which was not sanctioned by the UN. The SANDF and the SA Army predominantly take a manoeuvrist approach to conventional operations. Nonetheless, it is clear that there is a need to extend this stance into offensive peacekeeping operations.

Conclusion

The formation of a new South African military requires the creation of new conceptual models to achieve the objectives of a changing strategic environment. These models can be created using existing principles of war as a foundation. Such conceptual models for operational application must be proportional to UN conceptual models.

In order for operations to be effective, a suitable commander needs to be deployed in offensive peacekeeping operations. The commander must understand the makeup of forces available, the limitations and strengths of the UN, how to apply the available resources, and how to correctly implement the theories and principles of war in a peacekeeping setting.

One final question, however, remains. Can the strategic objectives of the FIB be achieved through tactical actions? If not, how will the strategic objectives be achieved and at what point will MONUSCO and the FIB be entering into counter-insurgency?

Chapter 6: Sustainable UN Peacekeeping Offensive Operations, Battlefield Clearance, Future Force Employment and the Strategic Peacekeeper

This chapter discusses various practical aspects of offensive peacekeeping Operations. These include the clearance of unexploded ordinance (UXOs), explosive remnants of war (ERW) and the ever increasing threat of improvised explosive devices (IEDs). The need for the FIB to consider its application in future operations with the constant threat of the reduction of forces and resources will be explored. This chapter will end by addressing the concept of the 'strategic corporal' in an offensive peacekeeping role.

UXOs, ERW and IEDs

With the ongoing change of the character of conflict, there has been an increased international focus on IEDs. The traditional threat of ERW has been further complicated by the preponderance of IEDs in war-affected countries. The UN is thus adapting its conventional approach in dealing with mines and UXOs to the complexities of asymmetric warfare. In this setting, IEDs have increasingly become the weapon of choice for non-state actors.

Earlier this year, United Nations Mine Action Service (UNMAS) celebrated its 20th year anniversary as the lead UN agency addressing the scourge of mines and UXOs. The Security Council and UN Department of Peacekeeping Operations (DPKO) have also taken novel approaches in combating spoilers with the deployment of the Force Intervention Brigade (FIB) as the first strategically mandated offensive peacekeeping force. This chapter discusses the interrelation between UN peacekeeping offensive action and the creation of UXOs, and its potential effect on local populations and existing humanitarian crises. A tactical and strategic analysis is then added.

The evolution of modern United Nations peacekeeping has resulted in a variety of complex operational situations with differing intensities of conflict. The use of force or the threat thereof to counter rebel groups and spoilers remains a fundamental part of peacekeeping, peace enforcement and prevention. The UN has adapted to changes in the operational environment with a number of innovations of which the deployment of the first offensively mandated force, the FIB, indicated a firm strategic resolve from the Security Council. The robust stance of the UN peacekeeping missions in Mali and the Central African Republic are also indicative of such approaches, as is the support role, which the UN has taken in the AU mission in Somalia. This book links the effect of tactical offensive operations to the further creation of ERW, which may increasingly contribute to a humanitarian crisis. One should not lose sight of the fact that the first principle should always be to do no harm.

The use of force is not new to peacekeeping, especially not in the Democratic Republic of the Congo.. Here, heavy tactical action was seen during the Congo Crisis in the 1960s and during the mid-2000s, as well as in Ituri and in and around Sake. The FIB's tactical victory over the M23 was another notch on the belt for the militarists in the UN. The attempt at offensive action did, however, not translate into any effective operation against the Democratic Forces for the Liberation of Rwanda (FDLR). Furthermore, the ineffective Disarmament, Demobilization and Reintegration (DDR) of the M23 and FDLR failed to capitalise on the gains made. These failures may have second and third knock-on effects, the extent of which remains to be seen.

The FIB operations made use of attack helicopters and ground forces. The weaponry included artillery, rockets, mortars, grenades and small arms. The ERW and UXOs, which came about as a result of the various operations, were never effectively cleared. Reports from FIB Explosive Ordinance Disposal (EOD) operators indicate that some attempt was made at clearing UXOs. However the complete clearance of the battlefields/areas of combat remains in question. As a result, in subsequent years, munitions from the previous combat were still found in and around Munigi, Kubati hills and Rutshuru. Reports from non-FIB EOD teams which deployed with UNMAS in 2015 indicated a considerable number of UXOs in the general area which were unmarked. Such ERW were brought to the attention of UNMAS through the local population and were addressed on a case by case basis.

The following question thus needs to be posed: when a UN offensive force is deployed in battle, what are the UN's responsibilities in terms of the post-combat clearance of UXOs? And should a combined UN force and UNMAS EOD team declare a given battlefield free from explosives following such combat? This is perhaps something that the UN DPKO and Department of Field Support (DFS) in combination with UNMAS should consider. UNMAS provides humanitarian and peacekeeping support to the UN as required. The onus remains with the Force and the UN operational and strategic headquarters to incorporate UNMAS in the battle plan and Concept of Operations. The question of whether there is comprehensive doctrinal guidance for UXO clearance post-offensive operations remains unclear.

Post combat doctrinal guidance is thus a necessity. This instruction should indicate the extent of the area to be cleared and declared free from ammunition and explosives as well as the timeframe for such clearance. Also to be incorporated is the relevant monitoring and reporting channels following a battle or skirmish. In order to ensure proper checks and balances, the following matter needs to be addressed: whether UNMAS officers should declare battlefields/areas where skirmishes have occurred free of munitions after the engagement when the tactical situation allows. Would the TCCs in combination with UNMAS personnel also be expected to map these areas? These are important considerations, especially with the advent of UN peacekeeping offensive operations and continued robust peacekeeping. There is also an international legal obligation under the Convention on Certain Conventional Weapons, Protocol V, for parties to a conflict to clear ERW after the conflict.

There appears to be a disconnect in understanding between UN military advisors and UNMAS staff with regards to what is happening in the field versus doctrinal and mandated requirements. Where the military advisors generally advocate a more aggressive approach to operations and combating IEDs, UNMAS tends to work within the scope indicated in the respective mandates and has a primary humanitarian focus. The military also tends to view IEDs pragmatically, with a need for a comprehensive strategy and suitable Tactics, Techniques and Procedures (TTPs). UNMAS– who are also fully operational at the sharp end –nonetheless has to consider the broader policy issues, standards and guidelines. In this regard, a technical manual is in production. While the operational situation is becoming more dangerous and complex, it is worrying to think that the strategic level is under what appears to be a self-imposed fog of war, which in all likelihood will take some time to lift.

The role of the armed groups (and opponents of UN peacekeepers) directly contribute to the creation of an unsafe environment, and thus require deliberation. But we should also consider how the UN indirectly adds to such issues. By not clearing ERW following FIB attacks, the Mission increases the chances of injury and or death to civilians which could lead to a lack of trust between the UN and the local population.

ERW can also be a source for IEDs. Various armed groups and non-state actors are increasingly using non-conventional tactics and terrorist methods in the execution of operations. The threat of such actors directly destabilises the security of missions. IED attacks are increasingly being applied in peacekeeping operations, posing a considerable threat to the local population and to the UN peacekeepers.

There is perhaps nothing that strikes more fear into the hearts of TCCs than the threat of IEDs. For a nation at war, the threat of IEDs is a regular occurrence and the death and injury caused by such weapons are part of the damage associated with the ultimate sacrifice of war. Peacekeeping in its many forms, is different to war fighting. There is a much lower national will and appetite for losses in peace operations. While IEDs are used as a means to achieve military and political ends there are also more neutral explosive threats in mission areas. ERW, mines and UXOs which often exist as the legacy of high-intensity operations, still present the greatest non-prejudiced threat to local populations. In this regard, UXOs pose a particular risk to children who often come into contact with them. These children do not understand their danger, and play with them, mistaking them for toys.

With the evolution of peace missions, UN forces have come into contact with more sophisticated armed actors. We have hence seen the manipulation of UXOs which are subsequently being developed into IEDs. The DRC has had an increase in IED attacks over the last few years. One such device was detonated in Goma in 2016. There have also been a considerable number of IED attacks in Mali and Somalia, just to mention a few missions. This increasing prevalence is a clear indication of the growing threat of such devices to peacekeeping operations. The threat is magnified by the availability of UXOs which can be modified into IEDs and should be seen as a growing potential security challenge. In this regard, the UN is obligated to ensure that following conventional operations, all battlefields are cleared of munitions. This will prevent the knock on effect of ERW modification into IEDs. In the grand scheme, this point can be regarded as a minor one. It is nevertheless important to create a culture of sustainable peacekeeping operations.

Another point to be considered is the way in which the UN selects its Troop Contributing Countries (TCCs), especially those who should form part of its peacekeeping offensive force. A key requirement should be the consideration of whether a given country is signatory to the various international laws and conventions on weapons and munitions. In this regard, the UN should have certain standards. For example, state X should be signatory to the Convention on Certain Conventional Weapons (CCW); and to the Convention on the Prohibition of Land-Mines.

The FIB comprises Malawi, Tanzania and South Africa as TCCs. Where South Africa is party to the CCW, Malawi and Tanzania are not. CCW Protocol V specifically addresses the scourge of ERW and the humanitarian problems that it causes and exacerbates. In this regard, some serious legal questions could be posed as to the requirements or specification of the UN when selecting TCCs, especially in an offensive role. The norms of a state dictates its organisational and doctrinal tendencies. If a TCC does not consider that being part to the CCW is important, how does that influence its approach to offensive peace operations? With regards to Protocol V, do ERW simply get left behind? And is it solely the responsibility of UNMAS to deal with the threat of UXOs?

The strategic issue of signing international conventions may be outside the direct control of the UN. The mission, however, has leverage over the FIB and other robustly applied forces in terms of their application. The South African, Tanzanian and Malawian battalions which comprise the FIB, are all deployed with a combat engineer platoon. Each platoon has limited EOD capabilities. These engineers can be used in conjunction with UNMAS to clear previous battlefields and areas where munitions were discharged. By doing this, they will ensure that the FIB does not aggravate an already appalling humanitarian situation.

Furthermore, the FIB combat engineers could become a force multiplier to UNMAS. Such an option would be similar to the use of military construction engineers, which fulfill a development role, in the building of infrastructure and a tactical role in the provision of force mobility. A similar function could be undertaken by the FIB EOD teams where they could assist UNMAS in the clearance of UXOs. This would need to be mandated and the correct organisational infrastructure, documentation and postings would need to be in place. These would include Status of Force Agreements, Concept of Operations, Mission Strategy, FIB Military Engineer Staff Officer, and liaison with UNMAS.

Chapter 6 has thus far discussed tactical as well as strategic elements in terms of offensive operations and UXOs. The international legal standards must provide the necessary guidance where field operations deal with the practical implications of IEDs.

When viewing conflict through the lens of IEDs, the normative framework includes international conventions, policies, mandates and TTPs. On a practical level – without sufficient decontamination of battlefields through UNMAS, contractors or military engineers – the battle may achieve tactical aims but also creates a humanitarian hazard to the local population.

The ultimate aim of the UN peacekeeping offensive action should be to promote security, safety and trust. The clearing of self-created UXOs should thus be compulsory. Furthermore, the clearing of UXOs will help win the hearts and minds of the local population. In relation to mine action and IEDs, the UN Secretary General Antonio Guterres said that a peace without mine action was an incomplete peace and people should not have to live in fear of dying after the end of a conflict (https://theowp.org/un-secretary-general-peace-without-mine-action-is-incomplete-peace/).

This section provides a microcosm for the concept of sustainable offensive operations. Where offensive operations are mandated by the UN, the SC should stipulate an objective of battle area clearance after a tactical action has been carried out. The clearance can be subject to the tactical situation. Nevertheless, the responsibility of ensuring that munitions are left behind, should lie with the mission and the military force deployed. The clearance of ERW in these situations should be carried out in conjunction with UNMAS and or other humanitarian demining (Non-Governmental Organisations (NGOs). Furthermore, it is proposed that a General Assembly Resolution be put forward. This Resolution should specifically call for governments involved in offensive operations to ensure battle area clearance following combat.

The potential impact of a reduced FIB in the DRC

If the FIB were to be decreased in size, the impact on MONUSCO will be substantial. If and when forces are reduced in size the FIB's role as the sharp tactical tip of the peacekeeping spear will be called into question. The ability for the FIB to project its power is largely shaped by its size and the resources that it had at its disposal. There has been considerable debate regarding the role and function of the FIB, its effectiveness and perhaps more importantly the political will in engaging the offensively mandated Brigade in combat. Another serious concern is of a structural nature and involves having this force situated within the confines of a slow moving peacekeeping infrastructure.

The reduction of the FIB will most likely lead to a reduction in its operational reach and influence within the mission. It will also create a less efficient response time to flashpoints and threats in far off areas. In order to compensate for a lack of numerical strength the mission the UN DPKO would have to allocate additional resources to the FIB. In so doing, the Brigade would be able to maintain its operational efficiency. To this end, an air cavalry method could be employed which could mirror the tactics used by the Americans in the Vietnam War. This method would of course require substantial air assets to be allocated to the FIB under the overall leadership of the mission. Where the American approach in Vietnam achieved success in tactical encounters, the political result was poor. Thus the operational application of the FIB must tie up with the political intent of the government of the DRC and the UN.

FIB Air Cavalry

In order for the FIB to be effective in a country as large as the DRC, it has to be able to negotiate difficult and diverging types of terrain. The mobility of the FIB should therefore be a fundamental concern for the UN so as to enable this force to execute its mandate objectives. The UN forces have largely become static with a slow response to flashpoints.

An air cavalry would gain the FIB valuable mobility, especially when the numerical strength of the force is reduced. The operational concept would be similar to the strategy of the central position from where the FIB could be rapidly deployed via helicopter into rugged, distant, austere and dangerous locations.

These types of operations are designed for staccato bursts of action which will address the threat of Armed Groups and spoilers on the tactical level. One has to realise that the Armed Groups are not conducting conventional operations. The FDLR, ADC and LRA are conducting raids, hit and run attacks and ambushes. These are typical of guerrilla/irregular/asymmetric warfare. The question thus is how to counter these attacks on the tactical level. The key is effective and proactive intelligence. This can be facilitated through Community Liaisons and forces deployed in local communities. Besides this, a hotline for locals where they could call in to the operations room would be useful. This, of course, will impose a logistical and manpower strain on the force. Any information from local sources would also have to be verified into reliable intelligence.

The information gathered should be processed into intelligence. From the intelligence, effective targeting should be done. A consideration of the protection of civilians and collateral damage is crucial. The rapid application of attack helicopters and the air lifting of troops to attack rebels and spoilers should provide the tactical answer required to provide a political and economic stability. These proposed operations are ultimately conducted by regular peacekeepers who are leaders in a complex environment. This is reminiscent of the idea of the strategic corporal which in many ways has become the strategic blue helmet.

Strategic Blue Helmets

US Marine Corps General Charles Krulak coined the concept of 'The Three Block War'. This is where soldiers had to conduct war, peacekeeping and humanitarian aid in three consecutive blocks. Krulak went on to discuss the 'strategic corporal', a concept that the soldier at the lowest level of command would have to take a decision that would have a strategic impact. In a similar way, peacekeepers have to take tactical decisions to impact complex strategic mandate objectives.

The conduct of peacekeeping operations is done by regular people, whether they are military or civilian. They are placed in a challenging context and with only the training and tools at their disposal. They are generally forced to carry out operations with limited resources. Civilians and soldiers work together but come from different worlds. Many soldiers do not understand the way that civilian peacekeepers work, and vice versa. There are often different ideas about professionalism, routines, discipline and other factors which renders cooperation more challenging.

The type and quality of soldiers used in peacekeeping missions should also be queried. Developed countries do not generally partake in peacekeeping operations. These nations often contribute forces to peacekeeping operations because of regional interest or financial reward. Whether soldiers from developed or developing nations, blue helmets are increasingly placed in complex security situations where they require dynamic training and inspirational leadership.

One could easily wonder whether the average foot soldier considers concepts such as the centre of gravity, OODA cycle and initiative, levels of war, decisive points and lines of advance. It may be even more difficult to imagine how the placement of soldiers in the field contributes to political change. An average blue helmet with conventional operations training, possibly some amount of counter-insurgency experience and some peacekeeping training is put in a complex security situation in a rugged location and asked to keep the peace. Blue helmets are overwhelmed by the lack of clarity – whether they should act as soldiers, policemen, civil servants or in some other role. This is further complicated by TCC's undisclosed political caveats. As a result blue helmets are often tentative of how to respond in certain situations as many times TCCs HQs issue orders which conflict with that of the UN mission HQ.

It is in the violence, boredom and confusion of peacekeeping, war and operations other than war that the corporals, sergeants, lieutenants, captains, majors and the higher ranks must inform the commander's decision. The commander must in turn provide guidance and advice on tactical matters to the political head of the mission. The Special Representative of the Secretary General (SRSG) or other political heads must then advise the SC, national political leaders, and other bodies of the progress of the mission. Much depends on the strength of personality of the force commander and SRSG, as well as the police commissioner. Where the political, military and police chiefs provide the strategic guidance, the execution of the mission is left in the hands of regular soldiers and civilian peacekeepers. Tactical decisions are thus taken by strategic

939

peacekeepers who must secure the conditions to achieve strategic objectives.

Friction is inevitable in the carrying out of operations by civilian and military personnel. Regardless of the considerations and thoughts of ordinary peacekeepers, these individuals are inextricably bound to the concepts which comprise the profession of arms or humanitarian work in conflict areas. Frustration for peacekeepers can creep in during the day to day life in small aspects, such as the unavailability of spare parts to repair vehicles. Irritation may occur at being in a hostile and uncomfortable environment.

Other factors that influence peacekeepers include keeping the same company for extended periods of time, having to eat preserved food, limited access to the internet and boredom. Many civilian peacekeepers deal with uncertainty, competition for jobs, planning rest and recuperation breaks, anxiety about renewal of contract, and fear in dangerous situations. The motivating factors related to self-actualisation such as promotion and pay increases disappear when there is an attack and fear of death becomes a reality. The strategic peacekeeper thus faces the outside world while fighting internal ambition and fears.

There is, however, a flipside to the friction ridden operational coin. When the slow moving peacekeeping ordinance machine finally delivers its spare parts, vehicles are repaired. When peacekeepers can embrace their surroundings, the mission can push forward. Then when soldiers meet the enemy and engage and win a skirmish or battle, they can experience courage, pride and jubilation. These feelings are as infectious as the initial fear that gripped them before the encounter. Thus the physical and psychological aspects of a military force are interconnected. They constantly sway like an out of sync pendulum where the ups and downs are not always proportionate in time, space and extremity.

It is therefore clear that the command has to take into account the logistical and material aspect as well as the psychological dimension. This is because these spheres of the military dictate and influence the cohesion and will of a military force. The tactical actions of the military must be understood by its civilian peacekeeping counterparts. The military commander must also understand the importance of the civilian peacekeepers who often have a more permanent and long lasting presence in the mission. In contrast, soldiers generally rotate in and out of missions every 6 months to a year.

In manoeuvre theory, pre-emption, dislocation and disruption are given as the three means of defeating the enemy and thus achieving victory. Surprise and speed are important in dislocating the enemy in terms of its material and psychological dimensions in the hopes of securing a decision. The means of achieving victory are thus hampered by friction, which is a very present reality for military operations. If the military victory does not achieve political objectives, then there is in fact no strategic victory but only a tactical one. Therefore, it is essential that civilian peacekeepers understand the plans and operations of the military. It is often the case where civilians do not understand the conduct and limits of operations.

In the case where there is confusion about the role of the military in peacekeeping missions, there will always be a less than optimal result. This may be further complicated by undisclosed caveats of TCCs which for the most part can be overcome by utilising forces with a political interest in the mission.

The speed at which a military advances in time and space is influenced by its command, morale and logistical supply. The pace of operations is thus influenced by the physical and the psychological spheres of the human condition. Operational pauses are taken at times where the logistical lines of an advancing force is stretched or where a military force can no longer sustain the advance for other reasons. The causes may include fatigue and demoralisation.

Manoeuvre warfare takes place on the operational level of war and thus involves large groups of soldiers. The movement and supply of these soldiers are dependent on the logistical support available. The planning of logistics for the movement and supply of soldiers is scientific. These logistics can, within reason, be calculated and planned for. The logistical planning for divisions, brigades and regiments is dependent on the funds and resources available to the mission. The limits of the deployment of forces and hence the extent of the physical protection of civilians is limited by the available logistics.

Military theory is frequently executed at the operational level of war. It can thus be used to provide ways in which victory can be achieved. Where offensive peacekeeping operation is complex, it is difficult for the military and civilian components to know what to do in each unique situation. This can be likened to a chess textbook in which it states what must be done to attain checkmate, but does not describe how the action must be carried out. The 'how' seems to be more enigmatic and certain commanders (chess players) have the ability to see what others cannot see and require a competent military force to execute their vision. Here, another important question can be posed: How could one achieve surprise on the operational level where the deployment of large groups of soldiers are known and mostly visible?

The answer, I believe, lies within the opponents who are engaged in the conflict. This dynamic can also be compared to a chess game.

In chess, even though you see your opponent's moves, you do not always know what will happen next. The development of chess from the opening to the middle game creates perceptions in the mind of the players of what they think will take place next. However, it is not always possible to calculate what will happen next. Most often, therefore, a chess game ends with a victor and a loser.

Let us compare chess to offensive operations particularly on the operational level. You can be deceived by falsely envisaging the future move of your opponent and thus surprise can occur despite being aware of where your opponent's forces are. This is related to self-deception. For example, if the FIB believes that it will not be possible for a rebel group to attack them, they may be caught unawares. This is related to a lack of training, intelligence, negligence, or ambivalence – or a combination of these elements.

Surprise is inextricably linked to the speed with which a military advances. Intelligence and counterintelligence are, needless to say, fundamental. Should an advancing force take an operational pause at an inopportune time, then the chances of achieving surprise may be compromised. With the FIB deployed in and around Beni without being able to successfully advance on the ADF, it has effectively become a garrison. As such, it has lost the initiative and has become a static target vulnerable to attack. When the FIB counter-attacks, the rebels are pushed back, but are not neutralised to the desired degree. In fact, counterattacks often result in minimal casualties.

Where a manoeuvre force becomes a garrison force, morale can drop and the forces may become complacent. The conscious reduction of friction through efficient logistical contingency planning and morale monitoring and boosting activities, can act as a force multiplier to the manoeuvre force.

The analysis of own and enemy centres of gravity should incorporate a psychological and physical sphere. If the centre of gravity is a headquarters or a person, these centres would both comprise physical and psychological dimensions. These dimensions as part of the centre of gravity would have to be dislocated to induce defeat and secure a decision for own forces. In the analysis of the enemy centre of gravity, planners should aim to attack the psychological and physical aspects. By neutralising the leaders of the armed groups in the DRC and by placing continued pressure on their support bases, the rebels will be more likely to surrender whether en mass or piecemeal. This would, in turn, create an opportunity for DDR.

The logistical and physical elements of warfare on the operational level can often be calculated. The application of these elements, however, constitute the art of warfare and are more obscure and leave space for interpretation. The application of physical and logistical resources in the attainment of surprise is fundamental and thus the physical and psychological are linked to the attack and in defence of the centres of gravity. The advance and attack should follow the lines of least resistance and expectation which echo the physical and psychological elements respectively.

CONCLUSION

This book is largely a product of my experience and study during my time serving in the SA Army and serving as a UN peacekeeper. I have as far as possible tried to give the best possible account of my ideas and thoughts on the topic of South African Army's future operations as well as UN offensive peacekeeping. The book is ultimately a work of military theory and links political and strategic objectives to operational and tactical aims. Much of the work in this book is limited to the contemporary strategic outlook of South Africa and current UN operations in the DRC.

I believe that developing a conceptual framework which is common to both a given TCC in a particular mission and the UN DPKO is ultimately a sustainable way to approach offensive peacekeeping operations. This will ensure the alignment of philosophies about peacekeeping and more successful missions. This book has focused on the SA Army, MONUSCO and UN offensive peacekeeping operations. I have thus put forward certain philosophical suggestions including Capstone and Operating Concepts for the SA Army and UN offensive peacekeeping missions as well as possible doctrinal and structural changes.

Conceptual Models

The SA Army

This book analyses conceptual models for the SANDF as well as the UN DPKO.

SA Army capstone concept should be the SANDF's guide for how to consider future conflict in a climate of uncertainty and complexity. The capstone concept will direct the capability requirements which will in turn fulfill the strategic priority of renewing the landward defence capabilities. The development of a capstone concept should thus be intertwined with the Landward Defence Capability Board and its respective teams.

The SA Army Capstone Concept is proposed as, 'operational adaptability: operations in a complex African battlespace.' The proposed SAACC within the future SAAFDSCS is linked to the operating concept. The operating concept should describe how a future army operates.

The operating concept addresses how an army will fight within the context of complex terrain and human complexity in the African battlespace. The SA Army Operating Concept put forward in this book is, 'winning in a complex African battlespace.'

The discussion of South African military conceptual models finds it's nexus between the continuities in the nature of war and the constant change in the character of war. The changing character of war questions the shape and form of the SA Army as well as the capabilities required for future operations. It is within this vein that this book considers the required future SAAFDSCS for the planning and understanding of future war.

The proposed concepts should be limited in their forward projection. Due to the continuous change in the operational landscape, the concepts must exist in fluidity. The capstone concept and operating concept can be created for current operations regarding FIB with a future view of five to eight years or the corresponding amount of years as is practicable. South Africa's application of military forces is shaped by the regional political requirements and UNSC. The use of force in peacekeeping operations is complicated by a lack of clear direction.

The SC's mandate of unilateral offensive operations is in many ways a throwback to the thinking in the conception of the UN Charter. However, the UN has until present not effectively defined offensive operations within peacekeeping doctrine. As a result, it is difficult to understand the character and limits of such operations. The decision of the UN to make use of offensive operations necessitates the DPKO/DFS to develop military strategic and operational frameworks to define and efficiently execute offensive operations.

It is suggested that the military underpinnings of combat operations should be clearly stated in the DPKO Capstone Doctrine and should filter down through to the manuals for Infantry, Engineers, Special Forces, Air Support and other military elements. The understanding of offensive operations through a common doctrinal lens will promote interoperability. There is a need for 'joint' doctrine which should clearly outline command relationships, subordinations and organisation.

The path of offensive combat operations is a complicated one. The UN should carefully consider this, due to the inherent difficulty of fighting under the banner of DPKO, and because of the challenging precedent that it sets on the political level, whether formally or tacitly.

In order to promote continuity between the deployments of forces in offensive peacekeeping operations, this work proposes the creation of a future peacekeeping offensive operations cornerstone and operating concept. This concept should guide the application of force in peacekeeping operations. The cornerstone concept should guide the UN's overarching philosophy regarding the use of force in peacekeeping and the operating concept should guide the way that UN military forces operate in offensive peacekeeping missions.

The proposed title for the future UN peacekeeping offensive operations cornerstone concept is, Adaptable offensive operations: neutralising armed groups in complex international contexts. A suggested title for the future UN peacekeeping offensive operations operating concept is Enabling protection of civilians through mobile operations in complex peacekeeping environments. The South African military capstone and operating concept should be proportional to the UN's concepts. This will ensure continuity in thought and operational application.

	Capstone Concept	Operating Concept
)PKO	Neutralising armed groups in complex international contexts.	Enabling protection of Civilians through mobile operations in complex peacekeeping environments
SA Army	Operational adaptability: operations in a complex African battlespace	Winning in a complex African battlespace

Table 1: Capstone and Operating Concepts

Doctrine and Command Structure

Apart from the conceptual constructs, this book goes on to suggest that the UN make a minor amendment to its strategic and operational command centres. The suggested amendment involves the inclusion of exclusively dedicated to mandated offensive operations. The personnel will assist the strategic and operational commanders in operationalising strategic objectives, facilitating CONOPS, and advising the SG and SC on critical failings, strategic options, challenges and combat mandates.

Ultimately, this book contributes to the study of UN offensive operations. It proposes a UN military strategic and operational framework, theoretical constructs regarding offensive operations (manoeuvre theory) and suggestions as to amendments to doctrine regarding offensive operations across the level of peacekeeping. This will assist TCCs in their preparation for offensive peacekeeping operations.

This work suggests that the UN make use of manoeuvre warfare theory as a broad approach to the conduct of offensive operations on the strategic and operational levels of peacekeeping. Furthermore, this study suggests that the UN's theoretical approach to war and offensive operations be highlighted in the respective doctrinal publications and manuals. Manoeuvre warfare theory recognises the importance of technology as well as intelligence, counterintelligence and technology.

Where offensive operations are conducted, it is important that the mission cleans up after itself. This book provides a microcosm for the concept of sustainable offensive operations. Where offensive operations are mandated by the UN, the SC should stipulate an objective of battle area clearance after the completion of a tactical action. The clearance can be subject to the tactical situation. The responsibility of ensuring that munitions are left behind should, however, lie with the mission and the military force deployed. The clearance of ERW in these situations should be done in conjunction with UNMAS and or other humanitarian demining NGOs. Furthermore, it is proposed that a General Assembly Resolution be put forward specifically calling for governments involved in UN offensive operations to ensure battle area clearance following combat so as to reinforce Protocol V of the Convention on Certain Conventional Weapons. Protocol V requires parties to a conflict to remove ERW following a conflict.

It is hoped that the suggestions and recommendations made in this book will prove useful to the SANDF and in particular the SA Army, the UNDPKO and the AU. Ultimately, we should not lose sight of our combined objective: to ensure the safety and security of innocent people in conflict areas.

References

Abilova, O.,&Novosseloff, A., (2016). Demystifying Intelligence in UN Peace Operations: Toward an Organizational Doctrine, *International Peace Institute*

Angerman, W. S. (2004).*Coming Full Circle with Boyd's OODA Loop Ideas: An Analysis of Innovation Diffusion and Evolution*(MSMIS thesis), United States Air Force Institute of Technology, Dayton, Ohio.

Angstrom, J., & Duyvesteyn, I. (Eds). 2005. *Rethinking the Nature of War.* New York: Frank Cass.

Angstrom, J.,&Widen, J. J. (2015). *Contemporary Military Theory: The Dynamics of War.* New York: Routledge.

Anon. (2016). *Europe's Paper Militaries: NATO Spending Still Shrinking.* Retrieved 17 September 2016 from:http://www.the-american-interest.com/2016/01/29/nato-spending-still-shrinking/

Anon. (2016.) *UN Charter Chapter VII.* Retrieved 11 September 2016 from: http://www.un.org/en/sections/uncharter/chapter-vii/

Anon. (2015). "Understanding the African Standby Force, Rapid Deployment and Amani Africa II". *Institute for Security Studies Media Toolkit*, November 2015.

Anon. (2016). *UN DFS, Contingent Owned Equipment.* Retrieved 13 September 2016 from http://www.un.org/en/peacekeeping/issues/fieldsupp.

Anon. (2016). *UN Meetings Coverages and Press Releases.* Retrieved 10 September 2016 from: http://www.un.org/press/en/2016/sc12307.doc.htm).

Anon. (2016). *Security Council Report, June 2016 Monthly Forecast: DemocraticRepublic of the Congo.* Retrieved 21 September 2016 from: http://www.securitycouncilreport.org/monthlyforecast/201606/de mocratic_republic_of_the_congo_11.php.

Anon. (2016). *What are the biggest defence budgets in the world?*Retrieved 17 September 2016 from: http://www.telegraph.co.uk/news/ uknews/defence/11936179/What-are-the-biggest-defencebudgets-in-the-world.html

Australian Army. (2009). *Army's Future Land Operating Concept: Adaptive Campaigning.* Canberra: Australian Army HQ.

Baker, D.,&Jordaan, E. (Eds). (2010). *Contemporary Counterinsurgency: Roots, Practices, Prospects.* Cape Town: University of Cape Town Press.

Barlow, E (2015). *Composite Warfare:The Conduct of Successful Ground Forces Operations in Africa.* Solihull: Helion.

Barnett, C. (2004). *The desert generals.* Edison: Castle Books.

Baylis, J. et al (Eds). (1987). *Contemporary Strategy.* London: Croom Helm.

Berdal, M., and Ucko, D. H. (2015). "The Use of Force in UN Peacekeeping Operations", *The Rusi Journal,160*(1).

Black, J. (2013). *War and Technology.* Indianapolis: Indiana University Press.

Blyth, F., & Cammaert, P. (2016). Using Force to Protect Civilians in United Nations Peacekeeping Operations. In Willmot, H., Mamiya, R., Sheeran, S. & Weller, M. *Protection of Civilians.* Oxford: Oxford University Press.

Boyd, J. R. (1976). Destruction and Creation.Unpublished manuscript. Washington.

British Army. (2010). *Operations, British Army Doctrine.* Andover: Army Publications.

Caldwell, D.R., Ehlen, J.& Harmon, R.S. (2004). *Studies in Military Geography and Geology.* Boston: Kluwer.

Cerami, J. R.& Holcomb, J. F. (2001). *US Army War College: Guide to Strategy.* Carlisle: Strategic Studies Institute.

Cheng, C.C.S. (1994). *Air Mobility: The Development of a Doctrine.* Westport: Praeger.

Clemmesen, M. H. (2017), Present and Future Command Structure: A Finish View. In De Coning, C., Peace Enforcement in Africa: Doctrinal Distinctions between the African Union and United Nations, *Contemporary, 38*,(1).

Coetzee, D., and Eysturlid, L.W. (2013). *Philosophers of War: The Evolution of History's Greatest Military Thinkers Volume 1: The Ancient to Premodern World, 3000 BCE 1815 CE.* Oxford: Praeger.

Cohen, E.A., and Gooch, J. (1990). *Military Misfortunes: The Anatomy of Failure in War.* New York: The Free Press.

De Coning, C. Aoi, C.,& Karlsrud, J. (2017). *Peacekeeping in a New Era: Adapting to Stabilization Protection and New Threats.* New York: Routledge.

De Vries, R. (1987). *Mobiele Oorlogvoering: 'n Perspektief vir Suider-Afrika.* Pretoria: Harman.

De Vries, R. (2013). *Eye of the Firestorm: Strength Lies in Mobility.* Johannesburg: Naledi.

Dorn, A.W. (2016). Smart Peacekeeping: Toward Tech-Enabled UN Operations, *International Peace Institute.*

Dos Santos Cruz, C.A. (2014). Amendment to SOP Military Engineering, *MONUSCO Interoffice Memo from Force Commander*, July.

Dos Santos Cruz, C.A. (2015). Employment of Force Engineer Assets, *MONUSCOInteroffice Memo fromForce Commander*, October.

Dos Santos Cruz, C.A. (2014). Policy for Executing Engineer Works in Support of Operations, *MONUSCO Interoffice Memo from Force Commander*, August 2014.

Doyle, M. W.,& Sambanis, N. (2006). *Making War and Building Peace: United Nations Peace Operations.* Princeton: Princeton University Press.

Du Picq, A.(2005). *Battle Studies.* (J.N.Greenly,.,& R. C. Cotton (Trans.). Retrieved 23 January 2012 from http://www.gutenberg.org/files-h.htm.

Ellis, J. (1995). *From the Barrel of a Gun.* London: Greenhill.

Esterhuyse, A. (2001). The Theories of Attrition versus Manoeuvre and the Levels of War, <u>Strategic Review for Southern Africa,</u>*23*, (2).

Fitzsimmons,S. (2013). *Mercenaries in Asymmetric Conflict.* Cambridge: Cambridge University Press.

Frantzen, H. (2005). *NATO and Peace Support Operations 1991-1999: Policies and Doctrines.* London: Frank Cass.

Friis, K. (2010). Peacekeeping and Counter-insurgency – Two of a Kind?, *International Peacekeeping, 17*(1).

Gal, R.,& Mangelsdorff, D.A. (1991). *Handbook of Military Psychology.* New York: John Wiley & Sons.

Galgano, F.A., & Palka, E.J. (Eds). (2011). *Modern Military Geography.* New York: Routledge.

Garcia, A. (2017). A Proposed South African Army Future Deployment Strategy ConceptSystem: The Capstone Concept and the Operating Concept, *SA Army Journal*.

Garcia, A. (2017). A Manouevre Warfare Analysis of South Africa's 1914-1915 German South West African Campaign *Scientia Militaria,45*(1).

Garcia, A. (2015), *Manoeuvre Warfare in the South African Campaign in German South West Africa During the First World War* (MA thesis). University of South Africa, Pretoria.

Gates, S., & Roy, K. (2016), *Unconventional Warfare in South Asia: Shadow Warriors and Counterinsurgency*. New York: Routledge.

Glad, B. (1990). *Psychological Dimensions of War*. London: Sage.

Gooch, J, (1996). "The Use of History in the Development of Contemporary Doctrine". Conference paper at a conference sponsored by the director of development and doctrine at Larkhill.

Gray,C.S. (2005). How has war changed since the end of the cold war? *Parameters*, Spring.

Gray, C. S. (2007). *War, Peace and International Relations*. London: Routledge.

Gray, C. S. (2012). *War Peace and International Relations: An Introduction to Strategic History*. New York: Routledge.

Guterres, A. (April 2017). UN Secretary-General: 'Peace without mine action is incomplete peace'. Retrieved from https://theowp.org/un-secretary-general-peace -without-mine-action-is-incomplete-peace/.

Handel, M. I. (1992). *Masters of War*. London: Frank Cass.

Handel, M. I. (1989). *War Strategy and Intelligence*. London: Frank Cass.

Harsch, M. F. (2015). *The Power of Dependence: NATO-UN Cooperation in Crisis Management*. Oxford: Oxford University Press.

Hayden, H. T. (1997). *Warfighting: Maneuver Warfare in the U.S. Marine Corps*. London: Greenhill Books.

Hoffstater, S. (2014). *South Africa at war in the DRC – The Inside Story, 22 August 2014*. Retrieved 21 September 2016 from: http://www.timeslive.co.za/local/2014/08/22/south-africa-at-war in-the-drc-the-inside-story.

Hoiback, H. (2013). *Understanding Military Doctrine: A Multidisciplinary Approach*. London: Routledge.

Holmes, R. (2001). *The Oxford Companion to Military History*. Oxford: Oxford University Press.

Holmqvist-Jonsäter, C.,&Coker, C. (Eds). (2010). *The Character of War in the 21st Century*. New York: Routledge.

Hooker, R. D. (1993). *Maneuver Warfare: An Anthology.* New York: Presidio.

Jablonsky, D. (1987). Strategy and Operational Levels of War: Part 1.*Parameters,* Spring.

Jomini, A. H. (2007). *The Art of War* (Mendell, G. H. & Craighill, W. P. (Trans.).. Rockville: Art Manor.

Jordaan, E. (2012). An Airborne Capability from South Africa from a Special Operations Forces Perspective. *Scientia Militaria, 40*(1).

Kainerugaba, M. (2010) *Battles of the Ugandan Resistance: A Tradition of Maneuver.* Kampala: Fountain.

Kasarak, P. (2013). *A National Force: The Evolution of the Canadian Army 1950-2000.* Toronto: UBC Press.

Kilcullen, D.J. (2010). *Counterinsurgency.* Oxford: Oxford University Press.

Langille, H.P. (2014, October). Improving United Nations Capacity for Rapid Deployment. *International Peace Institute: Providing for Peacekeeping (8).*

Lansford, T. (Ed). (2013). *The Political Handbook of the World.* Los Angeles: Sage.

Lawrence, T. E. (1935). *Seven Pillars of Wisdom.* London: Jonathan Cape.

Leonhard, R. (1994). *The Art of Manoeuvre.* New York: Ballantine.

Le Roux, L. (2007). *South African Army Vision 2020 Security Challenges Shaping the Future South African Army.* Pretoria: Institute for Security Studies.

Liddell Hart, B. H. (1941). *Strategy of the Indirect Approach.* London: Faber & Faber.

Liddell Hart, B. H. (1967). *Strategy.* London: Faber & Faber.

Lind, W. S. (1985). *Manoeuvre Warfare Handbook.* London: Westview Press.

Mahnken, T.G. (2008). *Technology and the American Way of War.* New York: ColumbiaUniversity Press.

Mrozek, D.J. (2002). *Air Power and the Ground War in Vietnam: Ideas and* Action. Honolulu, University Press of the Pacific.

Musashi, M. (2006). *Book of Five Rings*(Cleary, T. Trans.). London: Weatherhill.

NATO. (2010). *NATO Strategic Concept*

Neethling, T.,& Hudson, H. (Eds). (2013). *Post-Conflict Reconstruction andDevelopment in Africa: Concepts, Role-Players, Policy and Practice.* Tokyo: United NationsUniversity Press.

Olsen, J. A.,& Gray, C. S. (Eds) .(2011). *The Practice of Strategy.* Oxford: Oxford University Press.

Paddon, E. (2013). Peace Enforcement in Africa: Doctrinal Distinctions between the African Union and United Nations, *Rift Valley Institute*

Parker, G. (Ed). (1995). *The Illustrated History of Warfare: The Triumph of the West.* Cambridge: Cambridge University Press

Prakash, C. 2011. *MONUSCO Military Engineer SOP, Force Commander MONUSCO,* November.

Rich, P.B.,& Duyvesteyn, I. (Eds). (2010). *Routledge Handbook of Insurgency and Counterinsurgency.* New York: Routledge.

Roush, Gary. (2016). Helicopter Losses During the Vietnam War. Retrieved 13 September 2016 from: https://www.vhpa.org/heliloss.pdf

SA Army Vision 2020 Team. (2006). *SA Army Strategic Profile.* Pretoria: SA Army HQ

SA Department of Defence. (2015). *South African Defence Review 2015.* Pretoria: Government Printing Works.

SA National War College. (2010). *Campaign Planning Process*. Pretoria: SANDF.

SANDF. (2007). *Joint Warfare Publication 139: African Battlespace*. Pretoria: SANDF.

SANDF. (2008). *SANDF Military Strategy*. Pretoria: SANDF HQ.

SANDF. (1996). *Staff Officers Operations Manual*. Pretoria: SANDF HQ.

SANDF. (2009). *Joint Warfare Publication 137: Defence Doctrine*. Pretoria: SANDF.

SANDF. (2009). *Joint Warfare Publication 106: Peace Support Operations*. Pretoria: SANDF.

Shalit, B. (1988). *The Psychology of Conflict and Combat*. New York: Praeger

Simpkin, R. E. (1986). *Race to the Swift*. London: Brassey's Defence Publishers

Solberg, B. T. (2000). *Maneuver Warfare: Consequences for Tactics and Organisation of the Norwegian Infantry* (MMAS thesis), United States Army Command and Staff College, Kansas

South African Army College. (1996). *Operational Concepts: Staff Officer's Operational Manual, Part VII*. Pretoria: 1 Military Printing Regiment.

South African National Defence Force. (2004). The Principles of War, *South African Military History Reader.* Stellenbosch: University of Stellenbosch.

Shrader, C.R. (2009). *History of Operations Research in the United States Army.* Washington: US Army.

Smit, K. (2014). *UN Presentation.* Retrieved 13 September 2016 from https://www.vhpa.org/heliloss.pdf.

Springman, J. A. (2006). *The Rapier or the Club: The Relationship between Attrition and Manoeuvre Warfare*(MSS thesis), United States Army War College, Carlisle

Stearns, J. (2015). Can Force be Useful in the Absence of a Political Strategy? Lessons from the UN missions to the DR Congo, *Global Peace Operations Review*

Strachan, H. (2013). *Contemporary Strategy in Historical Perspective.* Cambridge: Cambridge University Press.

Strachan, H & Scheipers, S. (Eds). (2011). *The Changing Character of War.* Oxford:Oxford University Press.

Tzu, T.(2009). *The Art of War* (A. L. Sadler, Trans.)..Tokyo: Tuttle.

Tzu, T.(1994). *The Art of War* **(L. Giles, Trans.).** Retrieved 23 January 2012 from http://www.gutenberg.org/files/132/132.txt.

UK Army, (2012). *Joint Concept Note 2/12I Future Land Operating Concept.* Swindon: Ministry of Defence

UK Ministry of Defence. (2012). *Joint Concept Note 1/14 Defence Joint Operating Concept.* Swindon: Ministry of Defence.

UN DPKO/DFS. (2008). *Peacekeeping Operations Principles and Guidelines 'Capstone Doctrine'.*

UN DPKO/DFS. (2017). *Policy: Peacekeeping Intelligence.*

UN DPKO/DFS. (2012). *UN Infantry Battalion Manual.*

UN DPKO/DFS. (2015). *UN Peace Missions Military Engineer Unit Manual.*

UN DPKO/DFS. (2015). *UN Peace Missions Military Reconnaissance Unit Manual.*

UN DPKO/DFS. (2005) *Aviation Manual.*

UN Expert Panel on Technology and Innovation in UN Peacekeeping. (2014). *Final Report: Performance Peacekeeping.*

UN. (2012). Global Counterinsurgency Strategy. Retrieved from https://www.un.org/counterterrorism/ctitf/en/un-global-counter-terrorism-strategy.

UN. (2015). *High-Level Independent Panel on United Nations Peace Operations.*

UN. (2011). The Contribution of United Nations Peacekeeping to Early Peacebuilding: A DPKO/DFS Strategy for Peacekeeping. In *Police Peacekeeping and Guidance.*

UN Security Council. (2017). *Resolution 2348.*

US Army. (2001). *.Field Manual Operations.* Washington: US Army.

US Army. (2009). *Field Manual 3-24.2 Tactics in Counterinsurgency.* Washington, US Army.

US Army. (2014). *TRADOC Pamphlet 525-3-1 The US Army Operating Concept, Win in a Complex World 2020 – 2040.* Fort Eustis: TRADOC Publications.

US Army. (2009). *US Army Capstone Concept: Draft Version 2.7.* Fort Eustis: TRADOC Publications.

US Army War College. (2011). *How the Army Runs: A Senior Reference Handbook, 2011-2012.* Carlisle: US Army.

US Government. (2009). *Counterinsurgency Guide.* Washington: US Government.

Van Creveld, M. (1991). *The Transformation of War.* New York: The Free Press

Vego, M. N. (2007). *Joint Operational Warfare: Theory and Practice.* New Port: Naval War College

Vego, M. N. (1999). *Naval Strategy and Operations in Narrow Seas.* New York: Frank Cass

Vego, M. N. (2015). On Operational Leadership.*Joint Forces Quarterly, 77(2)*

Vicente, J. (2009). Toward a Holistic View of Warfare, *Empresa da Revista Militar,2(3).*

Von Clausewitz, C. (2006. *On War* (J.J. Graham (Trans.).Retrieved 23 January 2012 from http://www.gutenberg.org/files/1946/1946-h/1946-h.htm.

Vrey, F., Esterhuyse, A.& Mandrup, T. (Eds). (2014). *On Military Culture: Theory, Practice and African Armed Forces.* Cape Town: University of Cape Town

Wallace, J. J. A. (2013). Manoeuvre Theory in Operations other than War. In B.H. Reid (Ed.),*Military Power: Land Warfare in Theory and Practice.* New York: Routledge.

White, N.,& Henderson, C. (2013). *Research Handbook on International Conflict and Security Law: Jus ad Bellum, Jus in Bellum and Jus post Bellum.* Cheltenham, Edward Elgar.

Wodehouse, T.,& Ramsbotham, O. (Eds). (2000). *Peacekeeping and Conflict Resolution.* London: Frank Cass.

Young, T. (1997). *Command in NATO after the Cold War: Alliance, National and Multinational Considerations*, Carlisle: Strategic Studies Institute.